THE LAND AND PEOPLE OF PORTUGAL

Portraits of the Nations Series

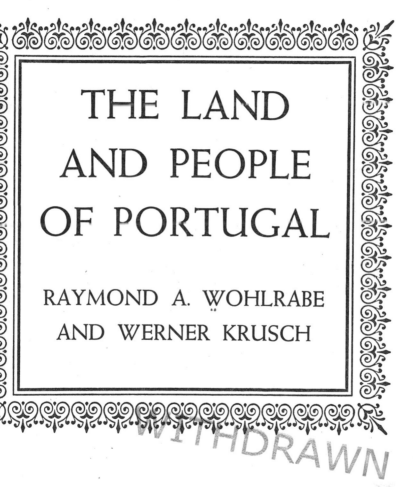

THE LAND
AND PEOPLE
OF PORTUGAL

RAYMOND A. WOHLRABE
AND WERNER KRUSCH

J. B. Lippincott Company
Philadelphia & New York

CONTENTS

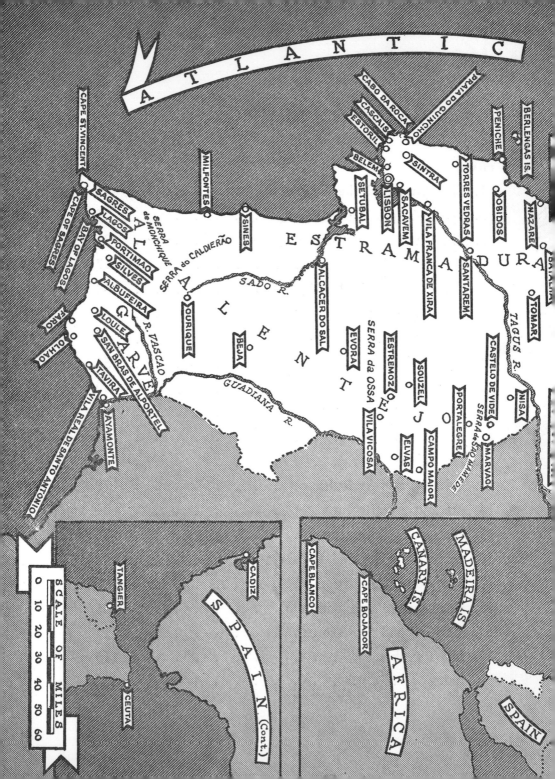

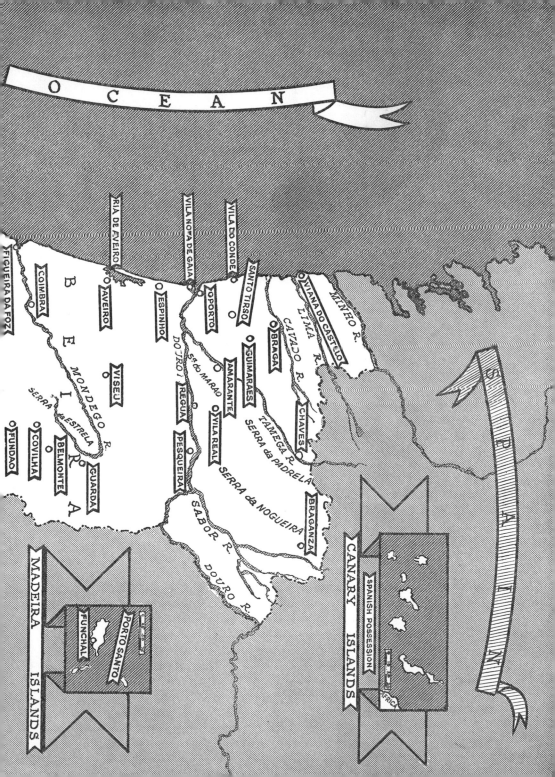

1 THE LAND AND THE PEOPLE

Portugal is a small land with a fascinating history and a friendly people. It lies on the western edge of the Iberian Peninsula, the most southwesterly part of Europe. The land slopes gradually from the fringe of the high plateau of central Spain to the seashore. The Atlantic Ocean which has meant so much to the life of its people and the existence of the nation lies to the south and west. More than four centuries ago Portuguese navigators ventured boldly into the water wastes of the Atlantic, the unknown outer space of their time. They shattered old established concepts of the world and the sea which were based upon fear and superstition. The water routes they charted tapped the riches of the lands they reached. The great colonial empire which was the reward for the efforts of her navigators has dwindled. What remains still places Portugal third among the world's great colonial powers.

No major natural barriers lie along the Portuguese-Spanish frontier. The determination of the people to be free has been the nation's sole bulwark against aggression. Their patriotism has served Portugal well. Boundaries drawn in the early periods of her existence have remained intact with little or no change to the present.

With its area of slightly more than thirty-five thousand square miles

Portugal is approximately the size of the state of South Carolina. Four hundred miles of coast line in the west extend from the northern boundary, the Minho River, to the high cliffs of Cape St. Vincent. In the south, from this cape to the estuary of the Guadiana River, is another one hundred miles of shore. All major harbors are on the west. Here also are the salt marshes, dune country, most important fishing villages and the long stretches of high cliffs pounded by spuming waves rolling in from the sea.

Most of the mountain ranges lie north of the Tagus River. They are spurs of the Pyrenees reaching into the land from Spain. These are the ranges where Celtic-Iberian tribes, the Lusitanians, built their hilltop strongholds, herded their goats and sheep and fought each other. The ridges run northeast to southwest. In the wine-producing provinces they are terraced for vineyards and ribbed with stone walls that separate small farm plots from each other. In the central regions are hills covered with forests of pine planted centuries ago to halt shifting sand dunes and to supply strong masts for sailing vessels built in the shipyards of Oporto and Lisbon. Near the northern border there are the short ranges like the Serra do Soajo, Serra da Nogueira and Serra da Padrela. Much larger, with peaks much higher is the more centrally located Serra da Estrela. Oak trees are common throughout the mountainous regions. Early tribesmen used the acorns for making bread. Today they are used to fatten the hogs turned loose in the forests in autumn. Both north and south of the Serra da Estrela are short mountain spurs. Some isolated ranges reach the coast. In the extreme south the Serra do Caldeirao and Serra de Monchique lie just inland from the Atlantic.

The Tagus and the Douro are Portugal's most important rivers. Both have their sources in Spain. The Tagus flows across the fertile plain where bulls are raised for the bullfight arena. Near its mouth is Lisbon, the nation's capital and largest city. The Douro, more rampant than the Tagus, moves swiftly through its deep valley in the mountainous wine country to Oporto, the second largest city. Picturesque river boats called *rabelos* with black or brown sails navigate some stretches of the Douro. They can be seen almost any hour of the day from vantage points on the hillsides where Oporto flanks the stream. Other major rivers entering the land from Spain are the Minho, Lima and Guadiana. The Cavado, Mondego and Sado rivers lie entirely within Portugal.

Though the country is small when compared with many of its European neighbors, there is a great diversity of climate, vegetation, people and customs. The northern and southern borders are only three hundred and fifty miles apart. The maximum breadth is one hundred and thirty-five miles.

In winter, blizzards dump heavy blankets of snow that remain until spring at the higher levels in the north. This wild region, generously cluttered with giant boulders and sparsely forested with clumps of oak, is hot in summer. Isolated homes are built of stone because wood is scarce. Stone shelters on wind-swept ridges offer goatherds and shepherds protection from storms. The severity of this winter climate of the north mellows toward the Douro valley and westward toward the sea. Showers are frequent and cool weather is common even in midsummer in the region around Oporto. Here, in Portugal's finest wine country, hillsides are not only terraced with grapevines trellised beside the stone retaining walls, but patches of corn grow luxuriantly in the plots between the trellises. Wooden-wheeled carts that creak along the winding roads are drawn by oxen with beautifully carved yokes decorated with leather and tasseled fringes.

Toward Coimbra, ancient university town on the banks of the Mondego River, groves of olive trees are more frequently seen. The air is less humid, the climate milder. Irrigation provides water where the soil is thirsty. Cultivated fields, orchards and woods of cork oak pattern the wide plain of the valley of the Tagus east of Lisbon. Near this city which legend claims was founded by Ulysses are such famous beaches as Estoril with holiday crowds and row upon row of canvas-topped cabanas.

Masses of pink blossoms festoon the branches of the almond trees in the province of Algarve in early February. Fields which become scorched and brown in late summer are carpeted with flowers. Figs and other semi-tropical fruits ripen during the peak of summer heat.

In this southern part of the land temperatures are highest. Algarve villages and homes, bearing strong resemblance to those of Moorish lands in northern Africa, are gleaming white in drenching sunlight.

The people of Portugal are generally short, sallow-skinned with dark eyes and hair. In the north, where the influence of Germanic tribes was strongest, there are some with light hair and blue eyes. Ethnologists do not agree on the ancestors of the modern Portuguese. Some claim they were the Lusitanians, the Celtic-Iberian race which offered such strong resistance to conquest by the Romans. But over the centuries other races mixed with these tribes of warriors, shepherds and hunters. Phoenician, Roman, Germanic and Moorish blood brought marked changes in traits. From this fusion of races came the Portuguese of today.

Each conqueror brought his culture, religion and language. The Portuguese language is more nearly the Latin of the Romans than that of any other European people. The Christianity of the Romans replaced the worship of ancient gods. It remained the religion even during the period when part of the land was under the rule of the caliphs of the Moslem world.

The Portuguese are a friendly people. They lack the haughty nature and, in most areas, the quick and violent temper of the Spaniard. They are a patient people. A large proportion of the nearly nine million inhabitants of Portugal work in the fields, the vineyards and the forests. Their love of fun eases the monotony of many tasks. Farm chores are often made the basis of a game or even a festival. Courtesy and good manners are common to both the cityfolk and the barefoot worker in the field. The will to toil is one of their greatest assets. Work on the farm is frequently done by methods outmoded by machines in other lands. Oxen and mules have not been replaced by tractors. Ancient methods of grinding grain, extracting the oil from olives, tilling the soil, harvesting and threshing are in common use.

Fishing, wine-making, the manufacture of cork products and the canning of sardines are major industries. Fishing fleets go as far as the Newfoundland Banks and the fishing grounds off Iceland to reap a harvest from the sea. Wine is stored in the cellars of Oporto wineries for proper ageing. Most of the world's need for cork is met by the vast quantity of bark stripped from the cork oaks that grow south of the Tagus. Porcelain, ornamental tiles, olive oil and canned sardines are exported to other lands. Salt is reaped from the coastal marshes and seaweed from the lagoons near Aveiro. In its two large cities new industries are being introduced.

Historians have thumbed through the precious documents stored in national archives and studied the charts and logs made by early navigators. They have found drama and adventure in the scripts on parchment hidden in ancient monasteries. Centuries-old legends and epic poems have added color. They have translated all of this into the story of Portugal's past.

Colorful figures have paraded across the pages of this history. The Lusitanian bandit leader Viriatus caught the attention of the civilized world of his time by leading his wild warriors in raids on Roman outposts. Christian nobles fought the Moor invaders when the tide of Moslem conquest reached the banks of the Douro River. Brave Alfonso Henriques united the forces that led to the birth of Portugal and to his becoming its first king (1140). The kings who succeeded him helped shape the nation and extend and strengthen its boundaries. They included Sancho the Colonizer, Alfonso the Fat, Dinis the Farmer and Pedro the Cruel.

Outstanding among the men who helped make Portugal a great maritime nation in the Middle Ages was Prince Henry the Navigator (1395–1460). Instead of enjoying a life of luxury at the royal court, he chose to gather about him the best astronomers, mathematicians and navigators of the time to probe into and chart the vast unknown world beyond the horizon of western civilization. His efforts led sea captains to sail beyond Cape Bojador on the African coast and develop a science of navigation that opened new worlds to trade, exploration and colonization. The fruits of his planning and determination brought wealth and power to Portugal long after his death.

In the Golden Age of the nation's history great discoveries were made. Bartholomew Diaz had sailed around the Cape of Good Hope, southernmost tip of Africa, in 1487. Then Vasco da Gama found sea routes to India and the Orient that cut drastically into the lucrative trade dependent upon camel caravans across the desert, Venetian ships across the Mediterranean and the route across the Alps. Eventually the expanding network of Portuguese sea lanes led to trading posts in Persia, Ceylon, China, Japan and other parts of the world. This Golden Age came to an end when a Spanish king annexed the land.

Spanish domination lasted sixty years. The Portuguese regained their independence in 1640. Immediate steps were taken to build again the empire partially lost to the English and Dutch while under Spanish rule. Brazil, a vast new source of wealth, was explored and colonized and its coffee, sugar, rice and diamonds brought to the mother country.

Near the dawn of the nineteenth century war raged across Europe again. In 1807 a French army crossed the Portuguese border, overcame the resistance to its progress, and swarmed into Lisbon. The capital of the nation was moved to Brazil during the period of occupation of Portugal by Napoleon's troops. With Napoleon's defeat the royal family and the government returned to Lisbon. Brazil eventually became an independent nation. In 1910 Portugal, after a revolution which resulted in the overthrow of the monarchy, took a republican form of government.

The red and green flag with its central shield commemorating the glorious past and symbolizing the five wounds of Christ still flies over Portuguese colonies in far-flung parts of the world. There are islands in the Atlantic and the big colonies of Angola, Mozambique and Guinea in Africa. Small colonies are in India and on the island of Timor. In the Far East is tiny Macao with an area of only six square miles, near Hong Kong on the edge of China.

Great changes have come to Portugal since the birth of the republic. Agriculture has been improved, although ancient methods of tilling the soil, threshing, grinding grain and doing many other farm activities are still in common use. Huge dams have been built on some of the rivers to supply hydroelectric power for industry and reduce the need of importing coal.

A president elected for a term of seven years and a prime minister run affairs of state. The land has been divided into eighteen districts although the older units called provinces with boundaries based on the natural differences between geographical regions have not been entirely discarded. Portugal, with a happy people eager to work and help in improving their country, is rapidly becoming an economically stronger nation.

2 BEFORE THERE WAS A PORTUGAL

Many races of people have inhabited the land we know today as Portugal. More than a million years ago Paleolithic man sought out the caves of its rugged mountains for shelter from storms and protection from animals. Ten to fifteen thousand years before the Christian era another prehistoric people came into the region. They were the people of the Neolithic period. They had improved upon the crude unpolished weapons and tools chipped from stone of Paleolithic cavemen. They also used the bow and arrow. The patches of grain and the fruit trees they cultivated gave them a greater choice of food. In the latter part of the period burial tombs called dolmens were built of huge stones. Many dolmens have been found in Portugal.

Two or three thousand years before the birth of Christ the first wave of a more advanced race swept into the northwestern part of the peninsula. These were the Iberians. Then came the Celts, swarming across Europe. In this southwestern corner of the Continent the two races fused to form five major tribal units. One of these, the Lusitanians, dominated the area that eventually became the northern and central parts of Portugal.

Other races came in the centuries which followed. They conquered the tribes that had preceded them and they brought new ways of life.

Some were eventually driven out by other stronger peoples. Each left tools, weapons and bits of pottery. Despite destruction and plundering by invading hordes, the ruins of habitations and settlements remain. These are clues by which archaeologists and historians have pictured the pattern of events in ancient times.

The Lusitanians and their neighbors, the Asturians and Galicians, were a Celtic-Iberian people. They possessed some traits and abilities we associate with a civilized race. The Lusitanians settled in that part of Portugal extending from the Minho to the Tagus River and in adjoining parts of Spain. A number of closely related tribes made up this wild, hardy race living in a land where life was a constant struggle to avoid starvation. They built their settlements on hilltops and encircled them with crude protecting walls. Here, according to early writers, they thrived on the flesh of their herds of goats and the acorns they gathered in the forests. From their hilltop strongholds they raided the settlements of more peaceful tribes in the valleys. Lusitanians are pictured as long-haired tribesmen wearing cloaks of scraggly black wool who pursued a life of hunting and warring on their neighbors.

Mariners from centers of civilization in the eastern Mediterranean ventured into the unknown Atlantic beyond the Pillars of Hercules. They knew about this militant hill people. It is claimed they were also known to the Greeks who sailed along the west coast of the Iberian Peninsula. The Greeks established settlements near the mouths of rivers as havens from storms and places to replenish their supplies of food and drinking water. About 1500 B.C. Phoenicians built a port on the present site of Cadiz in Spain and then, rounding Cape St. Vincent, they also built trading posts on the western shores of the peninsula. The people of Nazare and Aveiro, two of Portugal's well-known fishing villages, bear strong resemblance to the Phoenicians. Four or five centuries later the Carthaginians were believed to have visited the Portuguese west coast.

The legions of Rome made their appearance on the Iberian Peninsula shortly after dealing decisive blows to the Carthaginian Empire in the Second Punic War (218–220 B.C.). But their progress westward was slow because of the determination of the Lusitanians to be free.

By guerrilla tactics they harassed the Roman invaders at every turn.

In 150 B.C. a Roman army penetrated deep into Lusitanian terri-tory, burning and killing as it went. A large body of Lusitanians was surrounded. The Roman commander made glowing promises and con-vinced them to lay down their arms. Then he ruthlessly slaughtered them by the thousands. Some escaped. One was a warrior who later became known as Viriatus, a leader and a hero among his people.

The story of Viriatus is quite like that of heroes of other tribes who fought the Romans on the fringes of their sprawling empire. He had been a shepherd tending the flocks of sheep that foraged on the moun-tain slopes of his homeland. But a shepherd's life lacked the action and adventure he craved. He turned to hunting the wild game in the forests. This led to raiding the settlements of peaceful valley folk and robbing the inhabitants. His skill and cunning in raiding and robbing brought him many followers and led to bold raids on Roman settle-ments in Spain. In retaliation Roman legions were sent swarming into Lusitania and again a great body of barbaric warriors was surrounded. Again they were offered lenient peace terms if they would lay down their weapons. Viriatus reminded his people of their previous experi-ence with Roman promises and appealed to them to follow him. He miraculously turned defeat into victory and trapped large numbers of Roman soldiers. The invaders were sent scurrying to friendly territory.

For several years Viriatus and his army offered strong resistance to attempts at conquest. But success for the Romans came through treachery. In 139 B.C. several of the most trusted warriors of Viriatus were bribed to kill their leader. They carried out their mission while he slept.

After the death of Viriatus other leaders maintained resistance for some time. Finally Roman forces penetrated most of the land. They fortified Lisbon. They traveled north to Oporto and into what is now northern Portugal. It took two centuries to conquer the freedom-loving Lusitanians and several centuries more to Romanize the land and its people.

The Romans divided Lusitania into provinces and brought it into the empire. Great changes took place during this period. The Lusitanians came down from their mountain strongholds and were taught to till the soil. The ancient hilltop habitations and fortifications were destroyed by the conquerors. Roads of stone were built to link the towns and cities constructed by the Romans. Bridges that lasted for centuries were built across rivers. The people were taught the language of the Romans and they adopted Roman laws and religion.

Luxuries and wealth attained through trade with her colonies weakened the people that had extended the boundaries of the empire and brought power to Rome. When barbaric Teutonic tribes stormed the barriers along the northern and eastern frontiers they were successful in breaking through. Hordes swarmed into what is now northern Italy and France and swept south and west. In the early part of the fifth century the barbarians reached the Iberian Peninsula.

The Vandals crossed the Pyrenees into northern Spain about A.D. 409. Many historians claim they were the most destructive of the invaders, plundering and killing as they went. They invaded part of northern Portugal and swarmed across Spain. Another Germanic people, the Suevi, moved into the northwestern portion of the peninsula, and established the Suevian kingdom with its southern border the Douro River. The Vandals remained for only a few years. In A.D. 429 they had reached the Mediterranean shore of the peninsula, assembled a huge fleet and crossed into Africa.

The Visigoths followed the Vandals across the passes of the Pyrenees. Their leader, Euric, set up a Visigothic kingdom and, by conquest, included the kingdom of the Suevi within its boundaries. Under Leovigild (568–586) the power of their king was strengthened. During the reign of his son, Recared, who had become a Catholic, these Goths and the Iberian people joined to form a strong nation. Methods of agriculture were greatly improved. Industries and mines were developed. Trade with other countries expanded. Braga became one of western Europe's greatest cultural centers. An attempt was made to preserve and adopt the best that had been introduced by the Romans. Then the Gothic kingdom began to weaken because of division of power among selfish, ambitious nobles. Internal strife broke out. Across the Mediterranean in northern Africa a Moslem empire had grown in power and territory. Its leaders, ever watchful for an opportunity to invade Europe, saw their chance.

In A.D. 711 the armies of the Moors crossed the Mediterranean, gained a foothold in what is now Spain and pushed rapidly northward. Arabs, Moors, Jews and Berbers, a people some claim to be a remnant of the once powerful Vandals, conquered the Gothic kingdom. In Portugal they reached the Douro River.

With the Moslem conquest came an intermixing of races, an introduction of a new culture. The influence can be seen in many parts of southern Portugal. Houses were built in the Moorish style. Farming techniques known to the Arabs were adopted, some of which linger today. But many of the conquered people still held their religious beliefs and forms of worship under Moorish rule. They are called Mozarabs.

All of Christendom united to turn back the wave of Moslem invaders. They were halted near the borders of northern Spain. Confident that they had established themselves firmly in southern Europe, the Moors failed to mop up isolated areas in the mountains of northern Spain and Portugal where unconquered remnants survived. From these came the efforts that eventually swept the Moors from Europe.

3 THE BIRTH OF THE KINGDOM OF PORTUGAL

The Moors conquered almost all of the Iberian Peninsula at a time when there was neither a Spain nor a Portugal. Five centuries later in A.D. 1249 the last of the Moorish conquests in the western part of the peninsula had been retaken by the Christian armies. The first king of Portugal took a major part in the reconquest.

Invading forces of the Moors included many Moslem peoples. All were fervent believers in the teachings of the prophet, Mahomet. The Koran was their Bible. In the eyes of the Christians, they were infidels. Among them were the Arabs, a nomadic, desert-loving people. There were also the Syrians, Persians and the intolerant, fanatical Berbers. A great many Jews came with the invaders.

The first Moorish landing on the peninsula was made in 710. In 711 a strong force met with great success. In a battle meant to stem the tide of their advance, Roderick, the Visigothic king, was killed. This loss to the Christians was a signal for a larger army of invaders to attack. Resistance to their efforts dwindled rapidly and they became masters of most of Spain and more than half of Portugal. The northward thrust continued until it had penetrated the barrier of the Pyrenees and moved into what now is southern France. It was halted in a major battle near Tours in 732.

Military conquests are usually attended by ruin, destruction and injustices. Conquered peoples must submit to new laws. If they refuse, they must flee, hide or suffer. The Moorish invasion of the Iberian Peninsula was no exception. But the Moors proved to be quite tolerant. The inhabitants of the territory they took were permitted to worship in their own way and to retain most of their lands. They were heavily taxed and, of necessity, adopted Moorish ways. But they remained Christians and were known as Mozarabs.

At first the Moslem conquerors presented a strong united front in resisting efforts by Christian forces to recover territory lost. Abderrahman I was one of the Moorish leaders who did much to unite dissident factions and subdue rebellious leaders.

These regions the Moslems had won became independent of the Moorish empire in northern Africa and was called the Caliphate of Cordova. The city of Cordova became its capital with the luxurious palaces of the caliph and many beautiful mosques. In the land we know today as Portugal, the Moors formed a minority consisting principally of merchants and administrative officials.

The Mozarab majority in this western part of the peninsula acquired some of the culture and many of the ideas of the conquerors. The Moors had used irrigation effectively in their desert homeland for centuries. The *nora* or water wheel was brought with them to Spain and Portugal. It is a large wheel operated by an ox or a burro plodding in circles. Pots are attached to its outer rim. It lifts water from a cistern or pool and dumps it into a system of irrigation ditches. The nora is still in use in the Algarve and the Alentejo regions of Portugal.

The improvement of agriculture advanced rapidly in southern Portugal during the period of Moslem occupation. Rotation of crops to improve the fertility of the soil and the techniques of grafting to increase the quality of fruit-bearing trees were introduced. Plants like the lemon, orange and fig were brought by the conquerors.

The people were trained to new crafts and customs. Many were permanently adopted. The *azulejo*, a decorative tile, is an excellent example. In the expansion of the Moslem empire in Africa the art of making decorative tiles was learned by the Arabs from the Persians.

The Arabs used these tiles to decorate the inner and outer walls of their palaces and mosques. The designs on the tiles never included either animal or human forms since they were forbidden by the Koran. The patterns were entirely Arabic symbols. Mozarabs learned how to mix the proper proportions of sand, clay and water and how long to bake the mixture. They learned how to use salt to form the glaze and minerals to give color. When Christians reconquered the land, azulejos became very popular throughout Portugal but the figures of humans and animals were included in the patterns adorning them.

Goths who resisted Moorish rule fled to the mountains of Asturias in the northwestern part of the peninsula. The Moors made little or no attempt to take their stronghold. Failure to crush these people who remained independent was partly responsible for the events which finally drove the Moors from western Europe. These unconquered people chose one of their leaders known as Pelayo to be their king. From their mountain stronghold they made frequent raids into Moslem territory. The Asturias became the nucleus of resistance to Moorish control.

Cities held by the Moslems became centers of wealth and culture surrounded by strong fortifications. Their art, literature and scientific research surpassed that of any other part of western Europe. Then petty jealousies, personal ambitions, wars between various factions and treachery began undermining Moslem strength. At the same time Christian power centered in the kingdom of Asturias grew.

In the ninth century Alfonso III, king of Asturias, waged war against the Moors in several directions. The region between the Minho and Douro rivers became Christian territory. More land to the north and east was added and the small domain changed its name to kingdom of Leon. Both Galicia to the west and Castile to the east came under its control.

About this time a fairly large region in the kingdom of Leon became known as Portugal. The name had originated in *Portucale,* a little town that had grown up on the banks of the Douro in early times. Even before King Alfonso VI of Leon had met with considerable success in his wars against the Moors, the region around Portucale (now

Oporto) was called *Terra Portucalense*. Eventually it became the county of Portugal ruled by a count who, according to feudal custom, was a vassal of the king of Leon.

Alfonso VI ruled Leon and Castile in the latter part of the eleventh century. In his wars against the Moors he accepted the help of many an adventurous foreign knight. Some were from lands in parts of Europe we know today as France. Usually he paid for their services by grants of land or appointments to positions of power, a usual custom in the Middle Ages.

Henry of Burgundy was a nobleman who had served Alfonso faithfully. He was rewarded by being made count of Portugal and by being given a daughter of King Alfonso in marriage. Henry was ambitious and not satisfied to limit his control to the county the king of Leon had given him. He almost immediately expanded his domains to the south by taking over the neighboring county of Coimbra.

The castle in which a son was born to the count in 1109 still stands in Guimaraes in Portugal. He was named Alfonso Henriques. This was just three years before Henry's death. For some time the mother of the youngster attempted to rule. These were years of rampant intrigue that created dissatisfaction among the nobles of the county.

When Alfonso Henriques had grown to manhood the nobles his mother had so greatly antagonized rallied around him as their leader. They helped him become count of Portugal, the first who could be truly considered a native Portuguese. The young count's ambitions and determination quickly proved they had chosen well. He dedicated himself to the task of expanding Portugal and reconquering lands to the south still held by the Moors.

A decisive battle fought at Ourique in 1139 led Alfonso Henriques to make another daring decision. He declared himself king of Portugal and his lands and people independent of the kingdom of Leon. The king of Leon was beset by other grave problems that required his attention at the time. It was quite evident to Alfonso Henriques that his daring move would not be challenged.

The new kingdom of Portugal was not large and its status as an independent land still rested upon the ability of its young self-appointed king to strengthen it and maintain its independence. The northern boundary was the Minho River. Its southern frontier was the valley of the Mondego; beyond it, the lands were still in Moslem hands.

Alfonso Henriques deemed it wise to strengthen the position of his country by making it a fief of the Holy See in Rome. In 1143 this arrangement was completed, but not until 1179 was his title of king of the Portuguese given recognition by the pope. Castile had succeeded Leon as the dominant power in the Spanish part of the peninsula. He began intensive campaigns against both the Moors and the Castilians to increase the size of his kingdom. He moved southward toward the Tagus into territory which had previously been invaded by other Christian forces. By carefully planned strategy he took Santarem in the Tagus valley in 1147. His next objective was Lisbon, a port and stronghold held by the Moors.

Fortune smiled upon Alfonso Henriques. A large fleet of ships carrying crusaders bound for the wars in the Holy Land called at Oporto. The king immediately sought their aid. The fleet of ships carried soldiers from the German principalities, France and England. Their leaders agreed that a halt in the voyage to help Alfonso Henriques wrest Lisbon from the Moorish infidels was a proper project for crusaders. For weeks they camped outside the walls of Lisbon and battled to penetrate its fortifications. Dissatisfaction born of jealousies arose among the besiegers. But, eventually, in the spring of 1147 Lisbon was taken.

The capture of Lisbon was a great victory for Portugal's first king. But its fall left many problems to be settled. Lands he had added to his kingdom had been laid waste and towns were in ruins. The king launched upon a program of repopulating the devastated areas and again making the land productive. Many crusaders were given grants and colonists were induced to come to Portugal from other parts of Europe. Most of the captured Moors and many of the Mozarabs became slaves and took a vital part in the task of rehabilitation.

In nearly half a century the picture to the east of Portugal's frontiers had changed considerably. The Moorish leader in the area, had defeated King Alfonso VI of Leon and Castile at Sacralias in 1086. He had invited the Almoravides from northern Africa to assist him. In 1091 they overthrew the Abbadids. About the middle of the twelfth century they, in turn, were supplanted by another Moslem people from Morocco, the Almohades. These hostile Moors still held much of Spain and the Algarve region of Portugal and other areas below the Tagus River. They frequently raided the towns of the territory newly acquired by Alfonso Henriques. To combat this danger, the king permitted certain military religious orders to establish strongholds along the frontiers.

Alfonso Henriques did not live to see his kingdom reach far below the Tagus. But the kings who succeeded him carried the war against the Moors into these regions. It was not until the middle of the thirteenth century that the Algarve was taken and the borders of the land ruled by the king of Portugal were established and became almost the same as those of the Republic of Portugal of today.

4 GROWTH OF THE KINGDOM

The kingdom created by Alfonso Henriques needed strengthening. Regions devastated by wars had to be repopulated and the soil tilled. The flags of Moslem rulers still fluttered above strongholds south of the Tagus. Ships had to be built to carry raw materials, gold and the luxuries all Europe craved from distant shores. For two centuries after the birth of the kingdom of Portugal her kings worked toward building a strong nation.

Sancho I (1185–1211), son of Alfonso Henriques, followed his father to the throne. His principal concern was the defense of the realm against the Moslem Almohades. Their raids had penetrated to Santarem and Lisbon. He enlisted the aid of Danish, Frisian and German crusaders whose ships had put in at Oporto and Lisbon. But victories were usually followed by the task of rounding-up members of these forces intent upon looting the cities they helped to capture. In 1191 a strong army of Almohades wrested from Sancho much of the area he had recovered. Further help in his wars against the Moslems came through granting privileges to such monastic military orders as the Templars, the Order of Calatrava and the Hospitalers. They were permitted to build forts and castles in frontier zones as a bulwark against Moslem invasion. Sancho was also involved in wars with his Iberian neighbors—Aragon and Castile. The greatest contribution of his reign came through populating uninhabited or sparsely settled areas with people from northern Portugal and foreign lands. This won him the name of Sancho the Colonizer.

In this early period Portugal resembled other realms of western Europe. It differed from them in the absence of a large burgher or craftsmen class. Nobles who were vassals of the king were a powerful group because of lands they were granted and privileges they received. Equally powerful were members of the clergy. They also possessed vast holdings and special rights. Work in the fields was done by peasants and by Mozarabs and Moslems with the status of slaves. Portugal was a feudal state.

Troublesome times prevailed during the reign of Alfonso II (1211–1223), successor to Sancho. Military expeditions were made into Moslem territory to speed reconquest. There were difficulties with powerful bishops Alfonso tried to deprive of rights and lands. But some progress was made in setting up protection for the freedom of the individual and in limiting taxation.

Sancho II (1223–1248), was only twelve when his father died. After he became king he gave so much attention to military expeditions into the Algarve that conditions in Portugal went from bad to worse. Most of the Algarve was reconquered. At home, jealous barons warred against each other. The power of the king suffered. Sancho's brother, Alfonso, in league with the king's enemies, so undermined him that he fled from the country. This brother became King Alfonso III. During his rule there were wars with neighboring Castile. Reconquest of the Algarve was completed. The dialect generally used throughout the land became the Portuguese language.

King Dinis (1275–1325), faced problems entirely different. The reconquest completed and the wars between powerful barons practically ended, he looked for other ways to strengthen his kingdom and keep vassal lords occupied. He let it be known that improvement of the land would now win royal favor. Ability in war was no longer the sole qualification to gain recognition from the throne. Many large land grants made to the nobility and the clergy stood idle. King Dinis made every effort to break up these holdings and parcel them out to others who would till the soil and raise livestock. Because of his interest in agriculture he became known as Dinis the Farmer. The vast pine forests of Leiria, one of the most beautiful regions of Portugal today, is the finest monument to his efforts. He had ordered it planted to prevent shifting sand dunes from spreading inland from the coast. It also became the source of masts for the fleets of sailing ships which some decades later carried the Portuguese flag to far corners of the world. The Portuguese language replaced Latin in the writing of official docu ments and a university, moved later to Coimbra, was founded in Lisbon. Experts in navigation were brought from other lands to teach what they knew of the sea and ships to any who wished to enter upon a seafaring career. Monastic military orders whose grandmasters lived outside Portugal were driven out and the Order of Christ was created to replace them. Two triangles of territory, once Portuguese but long held by Castile, were recovered.

Despite wars with contenders for the throne in the decades following the reign of Dinis, much progress was made. Alfonso IV (1325–1357), sent out an expedition which rediscovered the Canary Islands, forgotten since ancient times. Pedro I (1357–1367), changed many of the methods of administering justice. His successor, Fernando (1367–1383), encouraged shipbuilding and the cultivation of the land. But, by marrying a woman not of royal blood, he brought serious complications into the matter of succession to the throne. The princess, Beatrice, born to them became the heir. When she was wedded to the Castilian king, the outlook for Portugal became grave because of the possibility it would become a part of Castile. Upon the death of Fernando, Queen Leonor complicated matters still further by her wish to rule as regent. Her ambitions so worried many of the nobility that they turned to John, Master of the Order of Avis, as a way out of the difficulty. The queen immediately appealed to King Juan of Castile for aid.

John of Avis, whose father was King Pedro I, looked to England for assistance in the expected battle with the armies of Castile. John of Gaunt, who was duke of Lancaster and an uncle of the English king, took an interest in the plea. An army of battle-hardened English longbowmen was soon on its way to help. John of Regras, a learned man, and the soldier, Nuno Alvares, strongly supported the opponent of Fernando's widow. The former persuaded the cortes, the legislative body or royal council, to elect the Master of Avis king of Portugal in 1385 and, late in the same year, the latter led his infantry against the armored cavalry of the Castilian king on the field of Aljubarrota north of Lisbon. It was a decisive victory for the Portuguese.

The assistance given by the duke of Lancaster led to a treaty between Portugal and England in 1386 which created an alliance between the two countries. It is still in effect. John also married Philippa, the duke's daughter. Naturally a favor was expected in return. Lancaster, with a claim to the throne of Castile, sent an army of English soldiers to invade the country. A supporting army of Portuguese was sent along by King John. But little came of this campaign. The English army was withdrawn to what now is southern France. But clashes between Portugal and Castile continued until 1411 when a treaty between the two brought peace.

King John I ruled almost forty-eight years (1385–1433). The many years of peace led his sons to yearn for a war of some kind. The three eldest were anxious to test on the field of battle many of the things their military education had taught them. King John had had enough of war, at least within the borders of Portugal itself. His sons pleaded for a conflict of some kind and suggested invading Morocco and capturing Ceuta. To satisfy his sons King John secretly prepared for such an invasion. The city of Ceuta was a rich stronghold near the entrance to the Mediterranean. To hide the real purpose of his preparations he pretended to be planning an attack upon Holland. When everything was in readiness the plague swept through the kingdom. Lisbon was in the area hardest hit by the epidemic and one of the victims was Queen Philippa. Despite her death, the great fleet sailed out of Lisbon harbor, its destination unknown even to its officers. Ceuta fell in the face of this surprise attack. The three princes, Edward, Henry and Pedro, were knighted by the king for their part in the battle. Ceuta was the beginning of a vast Portuguese empire beyond the borders of the homeland.

Portugal, as a power among nations, had come of age by the end of the reign of John I and the accession of Edward to the throne in 1433. Its borders had been definitely fixed through wars and treaties. In a world much smaller than that of today it looked to the sea. Beyond the horizon great areas of water wastes reached into an outer space of unknown ocean. Tales of catastrophes which had befallen men adventurous and fearless enough to sail to the west or beyond Cape Bojador on the African coast had thwarted the ambitions of navigators of the time. Superstition peopled this outer space with monsters and pictured it as the center of raging tempests. Maps showing latitude and longitude had not yet been invented. Arabs had found the astrolabe useful in the desert to determine the hours to pray in the mosques and the direction to Mecca. But the instrument needed improvement to adapt it for use in navigating waters far from land.

The western world of King John's time was small. Centers of population seemed far apart because travel was slow; modes of transportation primitive. Old theories had to be discarded; superstition banished. The kingdom of Portugal was on the brink of an era in which it was to play a major role in breaking the shackles of ignorance and fear.

5 PRINCE HENRY THE NAVIGATOR

Many ideas about the Atlantic Ocean and the world were shattered by Henry, third son of King John I and Queen Philippa. This prince, who probably never sailed beyond sight of the shores of his homeland, was born in Oporto in 1394. Power, wealth and prosperity which came to Portugal years after his death were due largely to the pioneering he sponsored, the discoveries his mariners made.

Near Cape St. Vincent, where grass and stunted juniper clings to the rocky promontory, was Henry's paradise. It is a lonely spot on the Cape of Sagres, close to this most southwesterly tip of Europe in the province of Algarve. Winds from the heart of the Atlantic howl across the barren land. Thundering waves send geysers of spume above the battered headlands where it faces the sea.

Peasant and fisherfolk of the region called the cluster of squat stone-walled houses *Vila do Infante,* the village of the prince. It was built to resist the elements. An observatory and shipyards were constructed at Sagres and Lagos. Skilled Italian navigators were brought to Sagres to teach young Portuguese at the nautical school how to handle ships, read charts and plot a vessel's course. The prince's men were brave and adventurous, willing to stake their lives against the terrors supposed to lie in the mysterious outer space of the fifteenth-century world.

Vessels built to probe farther and farther south along Africa's west coast were moored near Sagres. Others rode at anchor in the more placid Bay of Lagos to the east. The laborers who performed menial tasks were men banished to this desolate spot by Portuguese courts. Learned men, mapmakers, astronomers, mathematicians and geographers came to this research center to tell what they had seen, heard or discovered and to study the charts and books accumulated from all parts of Europe.

Prince Henry's ambitions stemmed neither from mere curiosity about theories and legends nor from the desire for personal gain. He cast aside the opportunity for a life of luxury and any thought of marriage. Early in 1417 he began making frequent visits to Sagres and chose the work to which he dedicated his life. Ceuta, perhaps, was the point that turned him from the palaces at Lisbon and Sintra to this desolate part of the Algarve. At the Moorish city he heard tales from dark-skinned Moroccan traders about lands to the south in the heart of Africa.

The prince was no hermit. His worth as a soldier, leader and diplomat had been proven. He had planned the construction of a huge invasion fleet in the shipyards of Oporto and had it manned and provisioned for the attack on Ceuta. The task was completed in record time. When the fleet sailed into the mouth of the Tagus it received one of the greatest ovations ever given by the people of Lisbon. He was among the first to land on the fog-shrouded Moroccan shore and to penetrate the fortifications of the Moslem stronghold. For their valor in battle against Ceuta's defenders, he and his two elderly brothers were knighted by King John shortly after the city fell. In this colorful medieval ceremony held in the mosque hastily converted to a Christian cathedral, Henry was made duke of Viseu.

Upon his return from Ceuta, the thoughts of the young prince centered on the problems of Europe and his native land. The expanding Ottoman Empire of the Turks sprawled across old established trade routes to India, China and Malaya from which came spices, silks and ivory. The ships of Arab traders were now bringing the precious cargoes to the Persian Gulf. Camel caravans carried them across the desert to be loaded aboard vessels of the great maritime city-states of

Genoa and Venice. Transport, profiteering, tolls and the hazards involved in crossing Moslem domains made nutmeg, pepper, cinnamon and silk very costly. Into the coffers of Alexandria, Cairo and Constantinople drained the gold of Europe. Turkish sultans were sending their armies to fight the empires of the West. All northern Africa, except Ceuta, was under Moorish control which extended across the routes through the Sahara over which gold came. The crusaders had failed to break the stranglehold of Islam.

Two solutions appealed to Prince Henry. If he could find Habesh, the Negro kingdom of the Christian ruler, Prester John, the encircling Moslem world might be thwarted. The story of Prester John's kingdom, based on fact and legend, was known throughout Europe. This legendary realm was somewhere in Africa. Habesh was pictured as a powerful nation with the sands of its river beds rich in gold. If he could find a water route by sailing south beyond Cape Bojador, the trade routes through hostile nations could be by-passed. Then cargoes from India would be carried by Portuguese ships. To Portugal would come much of the trade that had built fortunes and created lavish living for the merchant princes of Genoa and Venice.

Henry's men worked hard. The hope of making new discoveries spurred them on to greater effort. But navigators faced many difficulties. Sailing far from shore in their tiny *barcas* was hazardous. Larger vessels had not been built. Barcas had a capacity no greater than a hundred tons and only a single mast fitted with a square sail. The provisions and drinking water they could carry were insufficient for such voyages. In rough seas they bobbed and tossed. Charts were mere sketches of coastlines showing bays and the mouths of rivers, but nothing accurate regarding the distances between them. From the Arabs the use of the astrolabe and quadrant had been learned and the instruments had been improved. These were of little use to mariners in equatorial waters accustomed to fixing their position by the pole star.

In the first few years of the project planned at Sagres ships were sent into uncharted waters with orders to keep a log that might be of use in the future. But many fruitless voyages and very few discoveries were the reward for years of effort. Several islands of the Canaries

already known were reached. In 1420 Madeira, discovered and forgotten for more than a century, was rediscovered. There were landings
and explorations in the Azores. No water route to the Indies had been
found! Where were the spices and the rivers that flowed across sands
of gold! There was grumbling at home. Could not the money Prince
Henry was wasting be spent to better advantage?

The prince solved the problem of meager funds. He was Master of
the Order of Christ that had been created many decades before by King
Dinis. The possibility of reaching new lands whose peoples could be
converted to Christianity became a reason for diverting the funds of
the order to his project. His ships bore the red cross of the Order of
Christ and sailed under its flag.

In 1434, a year after King John's death, heartening news came to
the Sagres base. Gil Eannes, a navigator in the service of the prince,
sailed a ship far beyond Cape Bojador. He ventured into seas whipped
by the hot breath of the Sahara that carried desert sands far out from
shore. The uncharted course led through waters made dangerous by
strange currents and treacherous shallows. The Portuguese were jubi-
lant. Edward, elder brother of Henry, was king at the time. The
work at Sagres met with his enthusiastic approval. In 1435 Eannes
repeated the feat and sailed much farther beyond the cape.

Henry halted his work in 1437 to give his attention again to Morocco.
A younger brother, Fernando, now wished for an opportunity to win
knighthood on the field of battle. Henry lent his support to the idea
of a campaign against Tangier, near Ceuta. The invasion force was
small. The support at home that had been given the attack on Ceuta
more than twenty years before was lacking for this new venture. On
the desert the Portuguese were surrounded by Moroccans who fought
fanatically to annihilate them. During a truce, Prince Fernando was
sent as hostage to Salah ben Salah, the Moorish commander, in return
for his promise that the beleaguered army would be granted safe pas-
sage to their ships offshore. With the prince his prisoner, the promise
was forgotten. For years the Moors demanded that Ceuta be given
up as the price for Fernando's freedom. Handsome ransoms were
offered instead by the Portuguese but to no avail. Henry, determined

that the foothold gained in northern Africa should not be lost, stood firmly against accepting the Moorish terms. After several years of torture and illness in the prison at Fez, Fernando died and his body was hung from the ramparts of the desert fortress.

Voyages of discovery from Lagos and Sagres were resumed after the failure of the Tangier campaign in the period which began in 1441. Ships were designed with space for larger crews and quantities of provisions. They were lighter in weight, longer, with superstructures higher above the surface of the sea. Cartographers worked feverishly to put the information brought by returning mariners into new, more accurate charts.

Great progress was made in this period. Two of Henry's navigators, Nuno Tristao and Antonio Goncalvez, reached Cape Blanco on the African coast. Upon his return from a voyage in 1443 Tristao brought back a number of Negro captives. This aroused much interest among traders at home. Soon they looked upon Guinea, the name generally used at the time for lands along Africa's west coast beyond Cape Bojador, as a source of great wealth. To Prince Henry, converting these Negroes to Christianity would be an opportunity to win the favor of the pope and protection of Portugal's claims to the new lands discovered.

Lagos became a mart of the slave trade. Many documents point to the very humane treatment received by these people brought from Guinea. Others report the inhumane methods used in raiding the coastal areas of Africa to obtain the cargoes.

Maps were constantly being altered. What was thought to be the river of gold was discovered. Caravels had gone beyond Cape Verde by 1445. The Senegal and Gambia rivers were entered. The Cape Verde Islands were discovered. At the same time Portuguese traders bent on building fortunes brought more and larger cargoes to Portuguese slave markets.

During the last few years of Prince Henry's life his nephew, Alfonso, was king. He called upon his uncle in 1458 to accompany him on another invasion of the Moroccan coast. They captured the small city of Alcacer-Seguer. Prince Henry made the terms of surrender. The

Moorish inhabitants were permitted to leave with their belongings.

In the last years of his life the great prince seldom left his village near Cape St. Vincent. On those evenings when the winds from the ocean howled across the barren land he must have looked back over the years in appraisal. There were great successes, many failures, much yet to be accomplished to fulfill his plans. His mariners had failed to round the tip of Africa and find a water route for the rich trade in precious cargoes from India. But they had dispelled the imaginary terrors from the seas beyond Cape Bojador. His explorers failed to find the fabulous kingdom of Prester John. But they led the way to the vast land of Guinea rich in ivory, slaves and gold. His plan to colonize many of the islands offshore was a great success. His scientists and craftsmen had vastly improved the instruments used in navigation, made better charts, built ships far superior to any previously used. His work and planning had built the foundation of the Golden Age that was just ahead.

Prince Henry died late in the autumn of 1460. Today his body rests in its tomb in the Founder's chapel of the monastery commonly called Batalha on the road between Lisbon and Oporto. Here behind walls with parapets that form a delicate lacework of stone lie the remains of King John I and Queen Philippa in an elaborate sarcophagus. Along the wall are the tombs of the royal princes.

6 THE ERA OF GREAT DISCOVERIES

Not until the reign of King John II (1481–1495), was any serious attempt made to fulfill the dream of Prince Henry. King Alfonso V, nephew of the great prince, gave his uncle a free hand at Sagres. When Henry died, the king then concerned himself with the invasion of the domains of his neighbor, King Ferdinand of Castile. His interest in Africa never reached south of Morocco. The capture of Alcacer-Seghir, a success due largely to Henry's help, was followed by the taking of two more Moroccan strongholds, Arzila and Tangier, in 1471. These conquests gave Portugal a sizable empire on the African side of the Straits of Gibraltar. Guinea received little attention. Much of it was leased by the crown to a Fernao Gomez who built a fortune from the trade in slaves and ivory.

Historians look upon John II as one of the ablest monarchs in Europe in his time. He faced many problems at the outset of his reign. First he wrested from the nobility the power they had taken when his father was busy quarreling with Castile and making conquests in Morocco. Then, with great zeal, he turned to the task of continuing the work begun by Prince Henry. But historians do not agree on his rejection of Columbus. Some rate it a grave error; others, a wise decision.

Christopher Columbus, a Genoese by birth, spent many years in Portugal and served on ships that flew the Portuguese flag. What he saw, as a boy, in the harbor of his native city, was certain to create an interest in the sea. He sailed to the Guinea coast and the countries north of the Iberian Peninsula. He joined his brother Bartholomew in a thriving business selling maps and charts in Lisbon and married the daughter of a Portuguese noble.

In the Lisbon chart shop Columbus was constantly dreaming of the lands that might be reached by sailing westward across the Atlantic. He taught himself Latin so he could read about Marco Polo's travels. He studied Ptolemy's *Geographica,* a collection of maps and information compiled in the second century and unsurpassed for more than a thousand years. The map of the world by Toscanelli drew his attention. But in both of these sources there were errors. Ptolemy extended the land mass of Asia too far eastward. Toscanelli estimated the earth's circumference at only eighteen thousand miles. Columbus subscribed to both views. They were errors that made the Atlantic seem much smaller than it was and crossing it more of a venture than it seemed to be.

The Genoese mariner and map-seller was granted an audience with King John II in 1484. History gives few details of the meeting. The king was anxious to find the sea route to India but Columbus, he thought, must be just a dreamer. Learned men of the time no longer doubted the world was a sphere. But could India be as easily reached sailing west as by skirting the tip of Africa and then proceeding eastward? This man Columbus had no wealth. His demands were great. He wanted ships, men, provisions. If the venture met with success, then he wished to be knighted, made an admiral and viceroy of all the lands he discovered. Furthermore, he insisted upon a tenth of all the wealth such lands would bring the Crown! The king was dubious. But he was also shrewd.

The decision was postponed until a committee of learned men appointed by the king to consider the proposal, had time for deliberation. While Columbus waited, a ship was secretly sent out along the route the Genoese had given in describing the details of his plan. Violent storms almost wrecked the ship. It turned back to Portugal without success.

When Columbus received the king's answer, which the committee had decided upon mainly because of the gross error the applicant had made in calculating the distance to India, he looked for help at the Spanish court.

Discovery and the establishment of outposts proceeded rapidly in King John's reign. The resources of the Crown and the wealth from Guinea provided a large fleet and more pilots and scientists. This advantage Prince Henry had lacked. Experts in mathematics found a new way to calculate latitude from the position of the noonday sun and tables of declination they had devised. This invention was a boon to mariners accustomed to finding a ship's position by the pole star. They had no guide in waters where no pole star appeared in the night sky.

To make more secure Portugal's claim to lands her navigators had discovered, forts were constructed. One was built at Sao Jorge do Mina in 1482. Materials for its construction were assembled and marked in Portugal, then carried to the African outpost by ship to be set up. As a trading center and a place to provision ships Mina greatly strengthened the Portuguese position.

King John's navigators now put up markers more substantial than the wooden crosses Prince Henry's captains had used when they made discoveries. These were called padroes. Each was a column of marble blocks quarried near Lisbon. The base of the column was firmly embedded in the soil. On it were inscribed the date and the name of the discoverer. Each was topped by a marble block and cross.

Historians have found it difficult to build a detailed story of this period. Secrecy shrouded the plans and the reports of most voyages because of the prosperity that had come to Portugal from her newly found lands. It attracted the interest of other nations of Europe seeking to replenish treasuries scant of gold. Her neighbor, Spain, looked with great jealousy upon the success of the Portuguese. Also, historians lacked documents to provide the details. Records carefully guarded in India House in Lisbon were lost in the fire in the wake of the disastrous earthquake of 1755.

From meager sources it is known that several navigators made new discoveries for their king. Diogo Cao reached the river known to the Portuguese as the Zaire and to us, the Congo, on a voyage which began in 1482. On his return he brought a number of Negroes whose king had asked that they be taught Christianity. In 1486 another explorer returned from coastal regions beyond Mina with melegueta pepper and news of the kingdom of Prester John. In the autumn of 1487 came most welcome news. Ships commanded by Bartholomew Diaz were blown off course by a bitter storm. After sailing in unknown waters for days, Diaz reached Africa's east coast. This proved he had accomplished unknowingly what Prince Henry's navigators had hoped to do. He had rounded the southern tip of Africa. This was wonderful news to report in Lisbon on his return. But part of the glory that might have been his was lost. If he had continued on to India all the goals of the Portuguese would have been reached. His men, suffering from the hardships endured during the voyage, mutinied and forced Diaz to return. The chartmakers of the king were ordered to name the tip of the continent the Cape of Good Hope.

When Columbus reached Spain with news of his successes new problems faced King John of Portugal. His royal Spanish neighbors, Ferdinand and Isabella, became intensely interested in acquiring territories and establishing claims to lands discovered. Their appeal to the pope resulted in a papal bull, *Inter caetera*. It proclaimed Spain's right to all lands south and west of the Azores and the Cape Verde Islands, but made no mention of Portuguese rights. King John protested. Only by careful diplomatic maneuvers and threats of war did he win recognition of Portuguese claims. The Treaty of Tordesillas, signed in the summer of 1494, provided an imaginary line of demarcation extending from pole to pole. West of this line Spain had the undisputed right to discover and colonize. East of it, Portugal was free to build her colonial empire.

King John died in 1495. Like Prince Henry, he did not live to see the fruits of his efforts. His cousin, Manuel, followed him to the throne and reaped the harvest which the work of both these great Portuguese made possible.

One of the world's greatest ventures originated in Portugal early in King Manuel's reign. On July 8, 1497, a small fleet bearing the red cross of the Order of Christ on its sails and the royal standard of Portugal fluttering from its mastheads moved out of the Tagus estuary. Months of careful preparation preceded this historic day. The ships were especially designed for this voyage. They were built in the ship-yards near Lisbon. There were four. The two largest were the *San Gabriel* and the *San Rafael*. Vasco da Gama, a stern black-bearded mariner of noble birth, was in command.

Vasco da Gama was born in 1460 in Sines, a town surrounded by dune country near the coast in Baixo Alentejo. Like many a Portu-guese, while still a boy he left his native town for a life at sea. Ships on which he served took him to the hot coast of Guinea. Years of sea-faring fitted him well for the rigors of the venture on which he now embarked.

Tedious hours preceded the departure. There were conferences with the king and a last minute check with cartographers and cosmogra-phers. Sleep was had by neither da Gama nor his officers the night be-fore they sailed. It was spent kneeling in prayer in the mariners' chapel built in Prince Henry's time at the edge of the estuary. By a careful study of ships' logs and the eyewitness reports of members of the crews, historians have written a detailed account of this important voyage.

On the southward lap frequent stops were made. In quiet bays the ships were careened to rid their wooden hulls of barnacles and the bor-ing sea-worms that were a constant menace. At friendly ports water casks were filled, provisions replenished with fresh fruits and meats. Time was taken to study new regions and the people who inhabited them. At Mina, Bartholomew Diaz, who had accompanied da Gama down the west African coast, went ashore. Not until late November was the Cape of Good Hope rounded. Several days later the last padrao erected by Diaz was passed. By Christmas Day, 1497, the fleet had ridden out storms and sailed seventy leagues beyond this point.

There were both friends and foes in this world unknown to Portu-guese navigators. Strong currents and raging winds carried the ships far out to sea. Water casks were almost empty, food had to be rationed, and crew members sickened with scurvy. The Negro natives at several villages where the ships stopped were friendly. They were given little round bells and red caps in trade for bracelets of ivory, ornaments of copper and tin and occasionally an ox to supply fresh meat. The sultan of Mozambique welcomed da Gama, although he treated the gifts offered to him with contempt. Mozambique was one of the first Moslem cities on the east African coast da Gama visited. But the sultan's friendliness vanished the moment he learned his visitors were Christians. Ships of Arab traders were at anchor in the port with cargoes of spices, rubies and pearls. Their crews resisted Portuguese attempts to fill their water casks and a battle resulted. The little fleet lifted anchors and sailed north.

Word of da Gama's coming reached Mombasa before his ships arrived. The sultan shammed friendship and offered safe anchorage in the city's inner harbor. The offer was shrewdly refused. After nightfall Arabs armed with knives swam out to cut the hawsers of the ship nearest shore, boarded her, and fought a hand-to-hand battle on deck. The attack was foiled and the ships lifted anchor to continue northward.

Malindi, just a few miles from Mombasa, proved a peaceful haven. The sultan was friendly, gifts were exchanged, repairs were made and good advice was generously given. Pilots who knew the Indian Ocean were found. The Portuguese learned the time for reaching India was from April to September when the monsoons were blowing from Africa toward that land. They were advised to return during the December to February period when they blow in the opposite direction. Late in April, da Gama, with the Indian pilot aboard, ordered his ships to lift anchor and sail for Calicut on India's Malabar coast.

For over three weeks they sailed out of sight of land. The sails bellied under the force of the monsoon and waves hissed against the ships' bows. When Calicut was finally reached, it was found to be swarming with Arab traders. In the markets there was much trading in gold, silver, cloves, pepper, nutmeg, ginger, rubies and pearls. The ruling Hindu prince invited da Gama to his palace.

The days rolled by while da Gama tried to win the prince's sanction of trade arrangements between Portugal and Calicut. Arab merchants tried to prevent him. They had enjoyed a monopoly in this rich trade and had had the commerce of the Indian Ocean largely to themselves. Their little dhows built of planks held together by rope and catching the wind in sails fashioned from palm matting, had carried precious cargoes without competition. But, after two weeks of negotiations, da Gama set sail for home with his ships loaded with spice.

The return voyage was one of great hardships. Many men died of scurvy and fever. One ship had been destroyed on the way to Calicut. Another had to be burned since the death toll had not left enough men to navigate her. After rounding the Cape of Good Hope, Paulo da Gama, the commander's brother, became critically ill. One ship was ordered to continue to Lisbon while da Gama in the *San Gabriel* took his brother to the Azores in an attempt to save his life. Paulo died a few days after reaching the islands. In September, 1499, after a voyage that lasted two years, da Gama, discoverer of the sea route to India, reached home. All Lisbon turned out to give him a hero's welcome. He was given titles and honors by a grateful king.

A few months after da Gama's return a fleet of thirteen ships left Lisbon under command of Pedro Alvares Cabral. They were ordered by King Manuel to sail for India by the route da Gama had followed. For some unknown reason Cabral went farther west than had da Gama's fleet. By doing so he came to a large land mass; he could not determine whether it was an island or a continent. He named it Santa Cruz. Years later it was called Brazil. The lush vegetation, marshy coastal region and great rivers of this land discovered in April, 1500, was to be a very important Portuguese possession in years to come. There were no signs of spice, gold or rubies. But Cabral sent a ship back to Lisbon with his report. He recommended that it be made a way-station to break the long monotonous voyage for ships bound for India. Cabral continued his voyage. The big island of Madagascar off the east coast of Africa was discovered. He found the ruler of Calicut completely won over to the side of the Arabs.

In the ensuing years, battles raged between the ships of Arab traders and the Portuguese in the Indian Ocean and the Red Sea. But Arabs were neither the sailors nor the fighters that the Portuguese proved to be. Slowly their monopoly of Indian Ocean trade was broken and Portugal's power began to grow.

The discoveries made by da Gama and Cabral were of major importance in this great era. They were to have a terrific impact on the future of western Europe and the world. Portuguese navigators had dared to venture into the outer space of their time and had revealed a vast world of unknown lands. Portugal became the nucleus of a great colonial empire and a major world power.

7 THE PORTUGUESE EMPIRE

The reign of King Manuel was the Golden Era of Portugal's history. The nation which had been a small Iberian country attained the stature of a giant world power. All the planning and effort that began with Prince Henry's work at Sagres was now bearing fruit.

The extent of discoveries in this peak period of expansion will probably never be known. Details of many expeditions were strictly secret. Records kept in Lisbon were burned in the fire that followed the earthquake in 1755. Some historians believe Portuguese navigators reached Brazil before the landing of Cabral. John Fernandes, known as Lavrador, sailed with Cabot, the Venetian in the service of England. On a voyage to Greenland new territory was discovered that was named Labrador in his honor. Gaspar Corte-Real, member of a family of Portuguese explorers, found new lands along the shores of what we know as Canada. These discoveries led to the development of cod fishing on the Newfoundland Banks. Claims persist that some of these daring navigators were the first to go ashore in Australia. Antonio de Abreu sailed into the waters of the Pacific in 1511. Some pushed into the South China Sea. Still others worked up the rivers of South America. The sources of the Ganges and the Nile were found. Fernando Magellan, disliked by King Manuel, received no encouragement from his homeland. He entered the service of King Charles of Spain and was responsible for the first voyage around the world. Portuguese-born Cabrillo, also serving Spain, explored the southern California coast. Portugal had broken the barrier of superstition and opened vast new worlds for future exploration.

Control of the trade of the Spice Islands (the Moluccas) and the kingdoms fringing the Indian Ocean was King Manuel's great ambition. Fortified trading posts had been established by da Gama and Francisco de Almeida, who was made viceroy of Portuguese possessions in the East in 1505. Fierce attacks by Moslems trying frantically to hold their monopoly of trade with the East made the building of more forts and naval supply stations a necessity.

One of Portugal's greatest fighters, Alfonso de Albuquerque, succeeded Almeida as viceroy in the Indo-Asian area in 1509. By his strategy and planning Goa, on the west coast of India, was captured in 1510. In 1511 he took Malacca and established a fort to serve as a base for expeditions to the Spice Islands. Ormuz, on the Persian Gulf, also fell into his hands. But attempts to capture Aden at the entrance to the Red Sea met with failure. This prevented Albuquerque from closing completely the ancient trade routes from India to the Mediterranean Sea. But he built for his king a vast colonial empire of far-flung, fortified trading centers. Each had its sphere of influence over surrounding territory ruled by native sultans. Goa was his capital.

Courtiers at home were jealous of Albuquerque's success and power. They worked hard to undermine the confidence of the king in his faithful viceroy and eventually succeeded. The news reached Albuquerque when he was returning to Goa after an attack on Ormuz in 1515. At the time he was suffering from a severe illness. King Manuel had appointed Lopo Soares de Albergaria, his most bitter personal enemy, his successor. The blow was fatal. Albuquerque died while his ship entered Goa's harbor.

Both sides of the ledger must be examined to determine the true value of Portugal's sudden surge to great power. Lisbon was one of the most fabulous capitals in Europe. Her warehouses held stores of precious goods from the Orient. The shops along narrow streets were crowded with men bartering for silks, rubies, pearls and spices. Seafaring men from every corner of the world came to the city. Portugal had become the first country of western Europe to possess a large colonial empire. Her ships loaded cinnamon in Ceylon. They brought the harvest of cloves, the dried flower buds of a tropical tree, from Ternate and Tidore. In their holds bags of nutmeg, cases of camphor, frankincense, dyes, drugs and gems were brought to Lisbon's wharfs. Wealth came to the king and the nobility. Fortunes were built by merchants. Portuguese prestige among the nations of the world experienced miraculous growth.

Other factors tended to tarnish the glitter of this fabulous period. Ships were costly. Voyages to India and return required about two years because of the need of careening enroute, waiting for favorable monsoons, and gathering cargo. Ships built of wood are short-lived. Frequent replacements were needed. Storms and warfare took a heavy toll.

The strain of so great an expansion on a nation so small was tremendous. The population was far less than two million. With a tiny kingdom, an empire of trading posts so far away was certain to crumble. Little was being done to develop natural resources at home. Wealth that came only from overseas trade did not seep below the upper class. The cream of the nation's manpower was needed to build and man her ships, police the distant outposts of the empire, and war upon the Moslems. Seamanship learned in Prince Henry's nautical school at Sagres served the nation well. Improved instruments, maps and ships gave Portuguese navigators superiority over other maritime nations. So serious was the manpower problem by 1525 that convicts were being forced into service at sea.

Portugal's King Manuel was the envy of other European monarchs. He became King Manuel the Fortunate. The building of a vast empire was not his only goal. He also hoped he might marry Isabel, daughter of Ferdinand and Isabella, and perhaps inherit the throne of Spain. Isabel agreed to marry Manuel on one condition. He must drive out of Portugal all his subjects of Jewish faith. Manuel took steps to meet her demands. Forced baptism and persecution followed. Isabel's reign as queen was short. After her death, Manuel married her sister, Maria.

Upon the death of his father, young Prince John became king in 1521. In his reign the empire began to crumble. The cost of maintaining fleets and naval bases in the Indian Ocean began to drain the treasury. A resurgence of Moslem strength in Morocco brought the loss of all North African territory except the cities of Ceuta and Tangier. French pirates swooped upon Portuguese ships to loot them of their treasure. They attacked colonial outposts. The French set up colonies on the coast of Brazil, a land where the Portuguese took little interest in colonization.

Young King John III tried hard to hold together the empire he had inherited. He called upon the aged Vasco da Gama to voyage again along the fringes of the Indian Ocean. This time his assignment was not discovery. He was to put to an end the pilfering by appointed officials who had selfish ambitions at so great a distance from Lisbon. But the great navigator died shortly after his arrival in Goa in 1524. He also sent a fleet to survey the coast of Brazil, a land Manuel had not thought worthy of attention. He had Alfonso de Sousa establish a colony there in 1532. Then he divided Brazil into grants to be distributed to loyal, ambitious Portuguese. In 1549 he appointed a governor with his capital at Baia.

During the reign of King John III the Inquisition was used against heretics and Christianized Jews. The king's brother, Archbishop Henriques, became Inquisitor-General. During his term of office many innocent people met death by burning at the stake.

King John's death came in 1557. Since all of his children had died before him, his three-year-old grandson, Sebastian, was the heir. A regency was set up to rule until the infant king came of age. His grandfather's brother Henriques became the boy's tutor.

Young King Sebastian proved to be a dreamer who longed to bring his country the patriotic fervor that had made it an independent nation. He dreamed of great military ventures where the armies of Portugal could win glory on the field of battle. Conditions at home did not enter into his calculations. Barely out of his teens, he visited

Ceuta and Tangier. Moroccans were divided in their leadership. Upon his return to Lisbon Sebastian began preparations to invade and conquer all of Morocco. To bolster his forces he hired Spanish, German, Dutch and Flemish mercenaries. A huge fleet was assembled in the Tagus estuary. Early in the summer of 1578 the fleet stopped on the Algarve coast before crossing to the North African shore. Sebastian made an eloquent plea to his men and asked their support in his crusade against the Moslems. Then he sailed with his troops to the territory of the enemy. The huge fighting force Sebastian commanded moved into the desert country of the interior on the heels of the opponent. Their retreat was a form of strategy that had been used before against the Portuguese when Fernando and Prince Henry had invaded their territory. At Alcacer-Kibir they suddenly turned and held their ground. Hordes of Moorish warriors engulfed the Portuguese army. With fanatical fervor they poured onto the field of battle. King Sebastian was killed. Most of his men were either slaughtered or taken prisoner. Few managed to reach their ships and return to Portugal. Young King Sebastian's dream of an empire in Morocco had been shattered in one decisive blow. When couriers reached the homeland with news of the defeat, the nation found itself without strong leaders. The aged Henriques, now a cardinal, became king. But his reign was short. Upon his death in 1580, Sebastian's nearest relative, King Philip II of Spain immediately carried out his plans. His armies swarmed across the Portuguese border and, although the cortes elected the Spanish monarch their king, the land actually became a vassal state of Spain.

8 UNDER THE BRAGANZAS

High-sounding promises were made by King Philip II of Spain when he became King Philip I of Portugal in 1581. An agreement was signed for the purpose of keeping the two kingdoms separate. But omissions and loopholes defeated its purpose. The Portuguese had no desire to become Spaniards or be ruled from Madrid. Unable to find a strong leader of their own, they were unable to prevent Philip from carrying out his plans.

Three Spanish kings, Philip I, II, and III, were kings of Portugal in the sixty years which followed the meeting of the Portuguese cortes in Tomar. Their reigns make up what is often called the Period of Spanish Captivity.

Other European nations were harassing the far-flung empire of Spain. They now considered the Portuguese colonies to be a part of it and immediately turned their attention to India and the East. Trade that had flourished in Lisbon fell off. The Dutch founded their East India Company, took over the Spice Islands, and attacked Mozambique, Goa and Macao. Philip had assembled most of his great armada in the Tagus estuary preparatory to his attempt to invade England. The English, Dutch and French, during the sixty year period, turned their guns on Portuguese ships and colonies. The English found the opportunity to gain a foothold in the East an irresistible one. They attacked in the Persian Gulf and on the west coast of India. By the middle of the seventeenth century Portuguese power in the East had been shattered; Dutch control of Ceylon had taken the source of cinnamon. The Dutch had also invaded the coast of Brazil and took a part of the trade with the west coast of Africa.

In 1640 a group of Portuguese nobles saw an opportunity to gain independence from Spain. Spain had been weakened by the policies of her king. She was also at war. Her treasury was almost empty. These nobles asked the duke of Braganza, who had great wealth and owned the Azores and much of the land within Portugal itself, to be their king. The duke was not enthusiastic. He had no desire to assume the burden. But he finally gave his consent. The Spanish were driven out and the duke of Braganza was crowned King John IV.

The task that faced King John was not an enviable one. Portugal was poor. Wars had taken a heavy toll of her young men. Few crops were being harvested since lack of manpower and heavy taxes had brought agricultural development to a virtual standstill. Most of her ships were at the bottom of the sea. Her colonial empire and her markets were gone. Foreign powers which had been her friends had, under the Spanish captivity, become her enemies. King John turned his attention to improving conditions at home. He gave up any thought of recovering the empire in the East. Instead he pinned his hopes of improving the nation's finances on Brazil and the possessions in Africa. Border skirmishes with Spain dragged on for years. Not until after his death was a peace treaty signed with Spain conceding Portuguese independence in 1668.

Intrigue, schemes and plots found a fertile field in Lisbon for many decades after the restoration. To strengthen ties with England, Catherine, sister of Portugal's King Alfonso VI, was married to King Charles II. Before Charles agreed to the marriage, some very worthwhile gifts had to be included in her dowry. Among these gifts were Tangier and Bombay. Alfonso VI was mentally ill during most of his reign. His condition became so bad that his brother Pedro had to take over his duties. In 1683 Alfonso VI died and Pedro II became king.

In 1703 the Methuen Treaty was signed with England. It gave English merchants the right to sell their woolen cloth in Portugal and permitted Portuguese port wine to be sold in England with an import tax greatly reduced below the tax charged on French wines.

To preserve the balance of power in Europe, an alliance had been formed between Holland, England and Austria. The king of Spain had died. His heir had been chosen. It was the grandson of the king of France. This immediately brought on what is known as the War of the Spanish Succession. In the conflict Portugal took the side of the Grand Alliance.

Although the empire in the East which had brought great wealth to Portuguese kings was lost, a welcome source of new revenue was discovered. Explorers probing into the interior of Brazil found extensive deposits of gold. A few years later this good fortune was followed by the discovery of deposits of diamonds. Soon the royal treasury was in far better condition than it had been for many decades. It provided wealth for King John V, successor to Pedro II, to spend as he pleased. Much of it went for fine palaces, monasteries, libraries and the opera. Very little of it found its way to the great mass of the people. Again, like the wealth that came during the Golden Age, it was based, not on prosperity at home, but on products from overseas.

Jose I became king in 1750. During his reign one of the great figures of Portuguese history came to power. The king was an easy-going individual who left matters of state in the hands of his ministers. Because of this, Sebastian Jose de Carvalho e Mello rose rapidly as the strong man of the period. Carvalho is more commonly known by the title of marquis of Pombal which came to him late in his career.

Pombal's life was marked by scheming and quick, but carefully planned, decisions. He was born near Coimbra in 1699 and gradually worked his way into positions of great trust. When King Jose I needed a secretary of state for foreign affairs, he appointed Pombal to the post.

A great catastrophe that struck Lisbon and many towns of southern Portugal on November 1, 1755, helped speed Pombal's rise to power. A violent earthquake sent palaces, churches and homes crumbling to the ground in Lisbon. Fire broke out and swept through the ruined city. Huge waves swept shoreward from the Tagus estuary and brought greater damage and misery to the lower sections. Pombal immediately took charge. He took steps to prevent looting, to care for the injured and homeless, to bury the dead and to keep the government functioning. He lost no time in rebuilding the ruined city.

When Pombal won the complete confidence of the king he assumed the powers of a dictator. He disliked the Jesuits, their policies and the part they had played in affairs he felt were purely governmental. The order was banished from Portugal. He disliked the influence some foreign nations, particularly England, had over Portuguese trade and industry and took measures to correct this. Foreign interests had been draining gold from the treasury. He limited the power of the nobility. Ruthless blows were struck at those who opposed his policies. Many were sent to prison or exiled; some were beheaded. An attempt on the life of the king was used to further Pombal's efforts to eliminate opposition. But this ambitious minister left little improvement in the economic health of the nation. He was, like many other prime ministers and monarchs of the eighteenth century, what historians call an enlightened despot. Pombal was seventy-eight when King Jose died in February, 1777.

The princess who had watched the growth of Pombal's influence over her father became Queen Maria I. She had learned to hate him. His resignation was accepted immediately. One of her first acts was to release from the country's prisons the hundreds he had condemned to years of confinement. Many hundreds more had died in prison. Pombal, fearing reprisals from the Lisbon mobs, fled to his estate in the village which bears his name. There he spent his remaining years. He died in the spring of 1782. An elaborate statue of the marquis looks down today from its high pedestal in the park at the end of the mile-long boulevard leading into the heart of the Lisbon rebuilt from smoldering ruins according to his plans.

Wars, revolts and internal strife plagued the Braganzas. Turmoil on the Continent brought Portugal into many conflicts. These and the drain upon the treasury of governing colonies in the far parts of the world left little for bettering conditions at home. Pedro, prince consort, died in 1786. As husband of Queen Maria, he had been called king.

Late in the eighteenth century the French Revolution came as a frightening shock to many crowned heads. It uprooted the government of the most absolute monarchy in western Europe. The possibility of revolt within her own realm, the reports of the frenzy of the Paris mobs, the spread of radical theories of government worried Queen Maria. Some claim it was a major factor leading to her eventual insanity. Her son John, as prince regent, took over her duties. Portugal joined other monarchial governments in declaring war on the French republic.

Out of the French Revolution emerged Napoleon Bonaparte. In his plans to build a great French empire, Spain became first an ally and then a captive nation. In his desire to strangle England he turned his attention to neutral Portugal. His ambassador in Lisbon requested that Portuguese ports be closed to English ships and relations with England be terminated. Portugal refused. French troops massed in Galicia moved across the border and marched on Lisbon. Prince John and members of the royal family and the court boarded ships in the harbor. They sailed for Brazil just as the advance units of the French army entered the city on November 27, 1807. Soon the flag of France replaced the Portuguese royal standard above the Castle of St. George.

During this period of occupation by the French army in the Peninsular War, patriots continued to harass French forces. This and the assistance given by the English made the position of the French difficult. Eventually an invasion force under command of Sir Arthur Wellesley (later Duke of Wellington) drove them out.

Prince Regent John was asked to return to Portugal in 1813. Brazil had given the royal family a great welcome and during the Peninsular War had been the seat of the government in exile and the colonial empire. John was liked by his Brazilian subjects. He did not wish to return. He gave the colony the status of a kingdom on December 16, 1816. In the same year Queen Maria died. In the mother country the absence of John, who was now King John VI, caused much dissatisfaction. But he found life in Brazil more pleasant and far more secure.

In Portugal ideas born of the French Revolution had taken root. Events in neighboring Spain had encouraged their growth. The Spaniards had revolted and forced their king to give them some voice in government. Many Portuguese decided to work toward a similar goal. There were mutinies in the armed forces. A provisional junta or committee was set up to replace British Marshal Beresford who served as regent during King John's absence. Demands were made for a constitution. In 1821, after an absence of fourteen years, King John consented to return. Prince Miguel came with him. Prince Pedro, the eldest son, remained as regent in Brazil.

A meeting of the cortes was called by the junta. Its members voted to end many rights which the nobility possessed. They also wrote a constitution. It was placed before the king with the request that he promise to uphold it. But, while this body was making demands and forcing its royal prisoner to acquiesce, Prince Miguel was conspiring to restore the monarchy with its former absolute powers. He led an army toward Lisbon in 1823 and was joined by his father. The cortes dispersed and King John was again in control. To satisfy the radical factions within the kingdom he promised certain reforms.

Prince Pedro declared Brazil a kingdom independent of Portugal in 1822. The action increased his popularity with Brazilians. They made him emperor. Three years later King John recognized Brazil's independence.

A quarrel over who should be the successor to King John VI broke out in the Braganza family and led to the war which some have called the War of the Two Brothers. Prince Miguel received the backing of a very large number who favored the return to a monarchy unhampered by a constitution. So strong was his support he decided to make the attempt to secure the throne of Portugal for himself. Emperor Pedro I of Brazil, Miguel's brother, wished his daughter Maria to become queen. The whole affair was settled in 1831 when Pedro came to Europe, launched carefully planned sea and land attacks, and defeated Miguel's forces. Princess Maria became Queen Maria II in 1834. Miguel, who had been king through the support of his army from 1825 to 1834, went into exile and spent most of his remaining years in central Europe.

Queen Maria faced many of the problems that other members of the Braganza family had faced. The nation was weak financially. The civil war between her father and uncle had increased the national debt. Changes were made in the constitution. Religious orders were abolished. The trade in slaves was prohibited. Ministries changed often and a long civil war still further sapped the nation's strength. Upon her death in 1853 her young son became King Pedro V.

Pedro V was a boy of sixteen when he came to the throne. His father served as regent until he became of age. Pedro accomplished much in handling the problems of his reign which lasted until 1861. By a royal decree a time limit of twenty years was set after which all slaves were to be freed.

King Luis, brother of Pedro V, took little interest in the problems of the nation during his reign which began in 1861. In spite of his lack of interest, conditions in Portugal improved in some ways. A network of railroads was built to link the larger cities and towns. Trade increased sharply. But the usual problem of an empty treasury and lack of credit prevented any development in the colonies. Portugal, since the time of King Manuel I, had tried to hold more territory overseas than her population and her income could develop and defend.

Overseas territories became a major problem in the latter part of the nineteenth century. Other European powers began to take great interest in Africa. The right to a region is usually based upon a nation's ability to explore and establish settlements. In Angola and Mozambique, Portugal had made settlements along the coasts. Their purpose had been to facilitate trade in slaves, gold, ivory and spices. The hinterland had been disregarded. There had been little exploring and practically no settlements in the vast areas which she claimed. Angola and Mozambique were directly opposite each other with the unexplored, central Africa between them. The intention had been that this vast area would some day be explored and fused with her two established colonies to make one enormous Portuguese possession extending across the continent.

But other European powers had different plans. There was some exploration by the Belgians in central Africa. King Luis immediately sent expeditions into the area. But lack of funds hampered the work. Private capital was encouraged to develop trade with the areas. Through diplomatic channels an attempt was made to have interested powers sign treaties which would eliminate the possibility of any future dispute. Some powers did make such agreements. England refused. The English had looked longingly toward central Africa and had also dreamed of a Cairo to Cape Town railroad which would pass through the region. Under the leadership of Cecil Rhodes, who had a hand in a number of schemes involving Africa, England protested Portugal's claims. So determined were they to shut out the Portuguese, England threatened war in 1890. Portugal, realizing that opposition would probably mean the loss of all her established colonies in Africa, gave up her claim.

The power of the Braganzas dwindled rapidly toward the close of the nineteenth century. Brazil, which had been an independent nation for some time, deposed its Braganza emperor. Carlos, who had become king in 1889, lacked interest in conditions at home. Unrest spread throughout the kingdom. There were riots in Oporto in 1891. Republican strength increased and the leaders of the party fanned the flames of hatred for the monarchy. Propaganda against the king infiltrated the armed forces. Discontent assumed such proportions that Carlos gave Joao Franco, his prime minister, dictatorial power. The move intensified hatred of the government. On February 1, 1908, the king and the royal family were entering a carriage in Black Horse Square in Lisbon. Shots fired by assassins killed the king and Prince Luis and wounded Prince Manuel.

Young Manuel, who had no training for the kingship, fell heir to the throne. His reign was short. An uprising forced him to flee to Gibraltar where he and members of the royal family were taken by British warships to England. The rule of the Braganzas came to an end.

9 NORTHERN PORTUGAL

The Douro valley and the land reaching northward to the Spanish border are included in three of the former provincial units—Minho, Douro Litoral and Tras-os-Montes. Spain lies also to the east with the waters of the Douro forming the border in that direction. Oporto, Braga and Vila Real are the largest cities of the region.

The Minho country has picturesque hills and valleys and a coastal area with many quaint fishing villages. Its highways are usually flanked by stone walls or hedges. They traverse regions where acacia trees are a mass of yellow blossoms in the spring, forests are dark green with pines, and the blue clusters of hydrangeas add color to the most unattractive village. From the coastal communities fishing fleets voyage into northern European waters or across the Atlantic to the Newfoundland Banks in search of sardines and cod. Old fortresses stand guard along the Minho, the boundary between Portugal and Spain. Ancient monasteries, homes once owned by noblemen, churches and shrines are plentiful.

Viana do Castelo on the River Lima has historic buildings. The central square, the Praca da Republica, was laid out by King Manuel. An imposing Town Hall built in 1502 of granite blocks faces the elaborate fountain in its center. Late in August countryfolk stream into the city dressed in traditional costumes for the three day annual fair and festival of Our Lady of Agony. Praca da Republica and the narrow streets flanked by ancient granite-walled houses become crowded. The folk costumes are the most colorful in Portugal. The women and girls wear skirts of black stripes with red or yellow aprons embroidered with birds, flowers and hearts, a colorful fringed shawl, a bolero and all the gold or silver filigree ornaments they possess. There is singing, music and dancing. Solemn religious processions are a part of this great event. From wrought-iron balconies flowers are showered on the marchers in festival parades. Bullfights are held. There are folk dances and fireworks. In the evenings the songs and music of serenaders drift up from the River Lima.

There are Roman milestones in the vicinity of Braga. Five military roads radiated from the city in the period when it was known as Bracara Augusta. With the fall of Rome's empire, Suevian tribesmen moved into the Minho and they made Braga their capital. It was taken by the Goths in the sixth century and later fell to the Moors who held it until the Castilians drove them out. There are palaces and ancient churches. But most visitors come to see the shrine of Bom Jesus a couple of miles from the town. They climb the stairway with its mosaic patterns, chapels and statues grown gray with lichens, to the church on Mount Espinho. Some penitent pilgrims climb the distance step by step on their knees.

Portugal's first capital, Guimaraes, lies south of Braga. This center of the linen industry has many of its buildings decorated with fine blue and white azulejos. Its greatest attraction is the bulky, nine-towered, twelfth-century castle on a low hill back of the city. It was here that Alfonso Henriques, first king of Portugal, was born.

The roads around Guimaraes lead through vineyard country where the vines are trellised to look like trees. Along them plod the oxen wearing some of the most beautifully carved yokes found in Portugal. Their wide wooden surface is patterned in various designs including the Cross of Christ, hearts and flowers.

The northeastern part of this region is partly mountainous, but largely a plateau broken by a few fertile valleys. The rivers Tua and

Sabor cross the province and empty into the Douro. In the east the Douro forms the border with Spain and cuts a deep gorge in the flat countryside. This section is often treeless and very desolate, simmering in summer heat and, in winter, cold, bleak and blanketed with snow. Except on the east to west stretch of the Douro and in the extreme western part of the province there are few towns and cities. One, far to the northeast, is Braganza. It is an old city with the ruins of a castle King Sancho I built in 1187 and a large town hall.

The coats of arms of noble families are found emblazoned above the entrances to many of the old granite houses of Vila Real, a city founded in 1283 by King Dinis. There are large vineyards around the town and in the wooded country to the north. Chaves was once a Roman outpost. A many-arched bridge built during the Roman period still spans the River Tamega.

The vineyard country along the Douro is commercially the most important part of this region. The walls of the valley and gorge have been terraced to retain the rocky soil in which the vines grow. The whole region, from Pesqueira to Regua, is devoted to the production of port wine. Men and women start reaping the harvest deep in the gorge where the heat of the summer sun has brought about an early ripening of the grapes. As the season progresses they work higher and higher up the slopes. The grapes are carried, in large baskets strapped to the backs of the pickers, to the shallow stone or cement vats where the treading is done by men with bare legs and feet who work with occasional rest periods. To lessen the monotony the Portuguese always make a game of work. This phase of wine-making is no exception. Treading the grapes is often done to the music of guitars and accordions. After fermentation has started wine is drawn off into casks and then shipped either by rail or by picturesque square-sailed rabelo to the wine lodges at Vila Nova de Gaia. Here, in the cool caves of the cliffs on the left bank of the Douro opposite Oporto, it is aged.

Early each morning vehicular and pedestrian traffic swarms across the Ponte de Luiz. It is the high arched bridge, designed by the famous French engineer Eiffel, that links Vila Nova de Gaia with the heart of Oporto.

Oporto is a very busy, a very old and an unusually proud city. Below the cathedral, built where Teutonic Suevians once had a castle, the cries of vendors and shouts of children at play mingle with the noise of traffic. This part of the city is a maze of narrow streets. The windows of gray, slate-roofed houses clinging to the cliffside look down on the parade of rabelos and other river craft carried by wind or current on the Douro. Oporto followed no definite plan as it grew. Like many European centers of population, new streets and lanes were added wherever it was most convenient. Motor traffic circles about the equestrian statue of King Pedro IV in Praca da Liberdade. Avenida dos Aliados links this square with the park in front of the town hall and skirts a central section of mosaic walk flanked by trees, shrubs and flower beds. On a cliff ledge overlooking the Douro is the beautiful new Crystal Palace for sports.

Great events are a part of Oporto's past. When Romans came to the mouth of the Douro they found a small settlement surrounding the hill where the cathedral now stands. After the fall of the Roman Empire the Suevians took the town in the fifth century and enlarged it. Five hundred years later the Moors destroyed it. As Portucale, in the eleventh century, it was made a part of Terra Portucalense ruled by Henry of Burgundy.

The pride of its people stems from several historic events. When King John I was waging war to make Portugal an independent land, Oportans flocked to his support. The city was the birthplace of Prince Henry the Navigator. When he came to prepare for the attack on Ceuta the shipyards on the Douro turned out a fleet in record time. Oportans manned the ships. From the surrounding country the people brought their cattle to be butchered to provide provisions. They refused any part for themselves except the internal organs and thus became known as "tripe-eaters." For a long period laws forbade men of noble birth from residing in Oporto. It was also the center from which uprisings against Spanish rule in the seventeenth century and against the occupation by the French in the Napoleonic era began. In more recent times movements toward a more liberal government have frequently originated in the city.

Oporto has long been primarily a center of trade. For more than two centuries its wineries have supplied the port wine for England and its goldsmiths the filigree jewelry so popular in the land. Its churches are richly adorned with gold leaf, gold images and fine azulejos. In its museums are splendid collections of both fine art and the work of the craftsman. Its Ethnographical Museum has displays of folk costumes and oxen yokes from all parts of northern Portugal.

The Douro coastal area surrounding Oporto is a land of great beauty and quaint customs. Vineyards where the grape vines are trellised on trees, plots of corn, pine forests of Montemuro and Serra do Marao, the fashionable beach resorts and quaint fishing villages add to its charm. Historic structures in such towns as Vila do Conde, Leca do Bailio or Amarante provide reminders of its struggles and tragedies.

10 LISBON AND THE SUNSHINE COAST

Lisbon, Portugal's capital, sprawls over the hills on the right bank near the mouth of the Tagus. It is a colorful city of many moods. In the old quarters are labyrinths of narrow streets clinging to hillsides like the strands of spiders' webs. Along the river front by the Cais do Sodre the fishwives come, in early morning hours, to fill the flat-bottomed baskets they will carry atop their heads up steep hillside streets to fish-hungry Lisboans who eat little meat. They mingle with stevedores, commuters waiting to board the electric trains for the resort towns of Estoril and Cascais, and sailors from many lands. There is the peaceful Lisbon of the Castle of St. George looming from the highest hill. White peacocks roam in its gardens and visitors gaze on the noise and confusion of the city below its ramparts. There is the Lisbon of the June feast days of St. Anthony, St. Joseph and St. Peter when by the light of bonfires and lanterns street dancing lasts all night in the poorer quarters. Only after dark, aboard a ship or ferryboat, can one see the city aglitter with lights mirrored in the estuary Lisboans call the Straw Sea. To see the great metropolis in all its moods one must search in the shadows of the domes and spires of its churches, along its miles of mosaic walks and in the streets where stubby cable cars climb its steepest hills.

Sni-Yan

Partial view of Lisbon from Park Edward VII

Street in Nazare, Portugal's most typical fishing village

The Belém Tower in Lisbon — Manueline Balcony

Main Street of Coimbra

Dancing at the fishermen's festival in Nazare

R. A. Wohlrabe

Portuguese windmill near Fatima

Cork oaks and piles of the cork bark which is used
commercially are common in the area south of Lisbon.

Museum of the Royal Coaches in Lisbon

Sni-Yan

Famous painting by a Portuguese artist
in the Lisbon Museum of Ancient Art

Pena Palace, Sintra

R. A. Wohlrabe

At "Little Portugal" in Coimbra, child-size reproductions of all the different types of Portuguese homes and architecture become perfect playhouses in this children's park.

Fishboats near Aveiro laden with seaweed which is used as fertilizer

Fishboats on the beach at Nazare

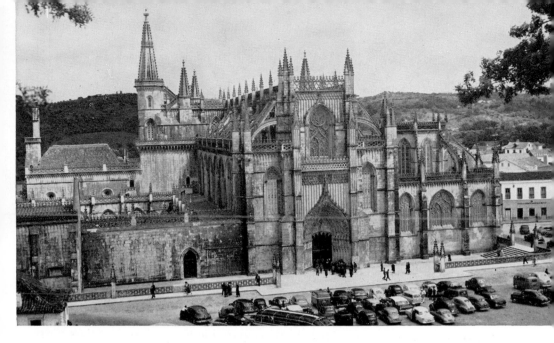

The ancient monastery at Batalha is now one of Portugal's national shrines.

Praca da Libertade in the heart of Oporto

The castle where Afonso Henriques, first king of Portugal, was born at Guimaraes

Fishermen of Apulia wear skirts when fishing

Foto Figueiras

New Year's Eve at Funchal, Madeira

Lisbon's history reaches far back among the centuries. Historians know Phoenician traders came to the Tagus estuary more than two thousand years ago. It was a haven for their galleys when storms changed the blue Atlantic to a black raging giant. They built the village of Olisipo which marked the beginning of Lisbon. When the Romans reached the mouth of the Tagus the city grew and was named Felicitas Julia. When their empire crumbled, barbaric Teutonic tribes moved in. These were defeated by Alaric, king of the Visigoths, who took Lisbon in 407 and it was held by the Goths until it fell to the Moors in 716.

The Moors converted the fortifications the Visigoths had built atop what is now the hill of St. George into a royal residence. They planted orange trees and exotic plants from northern Africa in its gardens. More orange trees grew in the little garden plots of the Alfama quarter below the ramparts to perfume the air with the sweet scent of their blossoms. Lisbon became a Moorish stronghold rich in treasure. In 1147 an army under Alfonso Henriques, first king of Portugal, with the help of an army of crusaders bound for the Holy Land, took the city from the Moors. Since then, except for sixty years (1580–1640), when it was held by Spain, it has remained under the flag of Portugal.

Lisbon was a busy city in the Golden Age of Portuguese history when sea routes were opened to all parts of the world. The vast wealth from silks, spices, ivory and slaves unloaded on its quays built pink villas on its hilltops. Churches were constructed with altars lavishly fashioned from silver and gold. Merchants from Venice, Genoa, the Low Countries and other parts of Europe came to trade. Many of the famous structures which remain today were built in this period of prosperity.

Most of Lisbon and a large part of its treasures were destroyed in the great catastrophe of All Saints' Day, November 1, 1755. Lisboans were at prayer in their sumptuous candle-lit churches when a violent earthquake rocked the city. Only in those quarters built on solid rock, such as Alfama, was destruction prevented. Palaces, churches and houses were destroyed. Fire followed the earthquake. The Tagus estuary rose in giant tidal waves to spread further havoc.

Estimates placed the dead at thirty thousand or more. Property worth one hundred million dollars was lost. The marquis of Pombal, minister of King Jose I, took over the city and began its reconstruction.

Ancient stuctures that survived the catastrophe of 1755 and modern buildings which have risen in the last few decades form the skyline of the Lisbon of today. The city is crisscrossed by wide tree-shaded avenues, narrow lanes, and alleys sunlight never reaches. Houses of pink, white and yellow cling like leeches to its hills. Artists try to capture some of its beauty in watercolors or oils. They prop their easels in side streets or in the shade of a tree high on one of the dozens of quiet viewpoints or *miradouros* for which Lisbon is famous. The city has a population of nearly eight hundred thousand today. The Tagus, its source in the high plateau of central Spain, winds through and around it for almost ten miles. Sleek ocean liners, gray men-of-war, cargo vessels, ferryboats and fishboats with brown or red sails ply the waters at its doorstep.

There is a legend depicted on Lisbon's coat of arms. It is the story about St. Vincent, the city's patron saint. His body was removed from Valencia, when that part of Spain fell to the Moors, and taken to the Algarve. The legend claims that ravens guided the boat carrying the body to Christian territory. The boat and the ravens are shown on the coat of arms. In Lisbon the black raven is a very common bird seen in every part of the city.

The river front is busy. Steps lead from the waters of the Tagus to the quays and the Praca do Comercio with its large statue of King Jose I in armor and plumed helmet astride his horse. The statue, cast from the bronze of melted-down cannons, was designed by one of Portugal's leading sculptors, Machado de Castro. The square has come to be known as Black Horse Square.

Three streets lead from Black Horse Square to the Rossio through the district called the Baixa. Traffic swirls about the Rossio. This square is often called the heart of Lisbon. Flanking it are the city's best-known cafés and, on its north side, the national theater, a building of simple design built in the days of the marquis of Pombal.

An obelisk in a circle north of the Rossio commemorates the liberation of Portugal from Spanish rule in 1640. This is the Praca dos Restauradores (Park of the Restoration). Extending to the north is the mile-long Avenida da Liberdade with its rows of flower beds and shade trees. On either side of the parkway are the big hotels, steamship offices and a few government buildings. At its northern end is a circle with the monument to the marquis of Pombal and the gardens of Parque Eduardo VII.

Vendors are as much a part of Lisbon as its monuments and historic buildings. The shrill cries of fruit and vegetable peddlers and the fishwives or *varinas* can be heard along the narrow streets of the Alfama or old town, the Bairro or high town and the Baixa district which parallels the river. The varinas are most picturesque with their baskets of silvery sardines or metallic gray swordfish atop their heads. They get their supply at the quay before most of Lisbon is out of bed and then, barefooted or with slippers, trudge from street to street shouting their wares.

Most of the old historic Lisbon was destroyed by the earthquake of two hundred years ago. But a great many historic structures remain. The Castle of St. George is to the right of the Rossio and below it is the Se or Cathedral, built in the twelfth century but reconstructed since. The little chapel of the Church of Santo Antonio da Se marks the birthplace of St. Anthony. The Aqueduto dos Aguas Livres, begun in 1729, oldest of the aqueducts bringing water to Lisbon from a source ten miles away, crosses the Alcantara valley. Well over a hundred masonry arches, some of them two hundred and fifty feet high, support it.

There is history and natural beauty along the banks of the Tagus estuary to Belem and along the coast to Cabo da Roca. The avenue leading westward from Black Horse Square skirts the site of the shipyards of King Manuel the Fortunate where the caravels that sailed on voyages of discovery were built. It merges into a wide highway beyond Cais do Sodre that leads to Belem.

The splendor of the dozens of royal coaches in the Coach Museum in Belem provides a picture of the pomp and fanfare when kings, queens and popes traveled in the period of the Renaissance. In what was once the riding school of a palace has been gathered together the largest collection of royal coaches on the Continent.

The most historic structure in this suburb of Lisbon is the Tower of Belem standing near the water's edge along the estuary. It was begun in 1515 near the spot where the fleets which opened the sea routes to distant lands set sail. The elaborately sculptured tower is now a monument to Vasco da Gama and one of the finest examples of the purely Portuguese style of architecture known as Manueline. In the old days it had a triple purpose—watch tower, prison and a fort to guard the harbor entrance.

The small chapel where da Gama spent the night in prayer before departing on his voyage to India once stood near the tower. In its place has been built the beautiful Church and Monastery of the Jeronimos. Inside is the tomb where rests the remains of the great admiral. There also is the empty tomb of Luis de Camoens whose epic poem, *The Lusiads,* tells the story of the voyages of the Golden Age.

Beyond Belem, picturesque resort towns dot the "Sunshine Coast." Each has beaches popular with bathers and wild stretches of shore pounded by giant waves that roll in from the Atlantic.

Wide formal gardens, a floral tapestry of color, reach from the small sandy beach into the heart of Estoril, world-famous resort town. Swank hotels, smart shops and cafés flank this carpet of flowers. The beach with its terrace cafés and rows of cabanas is crowded at all seasons. In Estoril's luxurious villas live many of the members of Europe's deposed royal families.

Cascais lies just a few miles beyond Estoril along the Sunshine Coast. Although cliff-top streets are flanked by pink and white hotels and villas, the beautiful bay is the scene each morning of great activity. The fishing fleet returns daily with its harvest from the sea and, in the market, fisherfolk are busy with the catch. One of the scenic attractions near the town is Boca do Inferno. Here an offshore cluster of rocks and natural arches whip the sea into a foaming rage that sends spuming waves sky high.

From Cascais the coastal road cuts through stretches of forest and sandy desolate country. Along the way is the wide beach at Praia do

Guincho and the westernmost point of the Continent, the cape called Cabo da Roca.

The hill and mountain country inland from the shore is a paradise of forest, flowers, quaint villages and mountaintop castles. This is the Serra de Sintra. Most famous of its villages is Sintra with winding streets, old villas and inns, a Moorish castle and Pena Palace. Trails through the forest are overhung with flowering vines and in the spring the mimosa and jacaranda trees burst into blossom. The last kings of Portugal lived in Pena Palace high on a hilltop above Sintra reached by a steep winding road through forests of pine and oak. The road crosses a drawbridge of the castle into a cobblestoned courtyard below its gray walls and towers. Guides take visitors through the lavishly furnished rooms, the little chapel where the wind whistles and whines, the Chinese room, and the room decorated in Meissen ware. Below the castle is the forest lake stocked with carp. From the palace windows are splendid views of the statue of a medieval knight high on a nearby mountain ridge and, on another, a huge cross.

The country around Lisbon is one of the most beautiful regions in Portugal. Its beauty reaches its peak in spring when wild flowers carpet the meadows and in many villages spring festivals with flower battles, folk dances and music are major events.

11 THE ALENTEJO

The rolling plains of the Alentejo reach southward from the Tagus River to the rugged hills of the northern border of the Algarve. They are the wheat lands of Portugal, broken by low ranges, hill country and isolated mounds. In the east they touch the mountains along the Spanish border. Here are the ancient walled towns where watchmen in castle towers warned when danger approached. Armies that came from the east to conquer used the valleys and plains of the Alentejo as their invasion route. In the west land tapers into the rice fields, the salt marshes and the sea. This once largest province of Portugal has been divided in recent years. The upper portion is now Alto Alentejo; the lower part, Baixo Alentejo.

This is a land where small towns and villages are far apart and peasants toil from sunup to sundown tilling the soil and harvesting crops. They strip the bark from the cork oaks of forests and pick olives, plums and almonds. Swineherds watch over the black pigs that root for acorns. Shepherds in long fustian capes guard flocks of sheep in the hill country. Some harvest salt from the sea near the mouth of the Sado. By mule cart they go to the fairs in the larger towns to buy from traveling merchants who have set up their stalls and spread their wares in the market place.

In the foothills and mountain ranges in the northeast are the citadels where time and thoughtless destruction by man have not erased the relics of the past. Mule carts, burros and oxen climb the steep cobblestoned streets. Centuries ago these same streets echoed the hoofbeats of horses and clatter of royal coaches. Their old convents, churches and palaces are adorned with tinted tiles picturing events of the past. In some towns historic buildings are now used as offices and barracks. Picturesque old chimneys poke above white houses with wrought iron window grills and balconies. The coats of arms of aristocratic families still are emblazoned on the walls of castles and town mansions. These ancient strongholds are sparsely scattered along the Serra de Sao Mamede and the more southerly Serra da Ossa.

Elvas, on its steep hill overlooking the plain, is one of the largest, busiest and most romantic of these old walled cities. Atop the hill is the castle. Below it are huddled the houses, glaring white, within the walls and moats that encircle the town. Inside the main gate one discovers a maze of narrow winding streets crowded with townfolk, peasants and soldiers. From ramparts and towers there are splendid views across the plains which are brown, yellow, or green, depending upon the season. In the churches is a wealth of sixteenth and seventeenth century tiles, paintings and images. The aqueduct built near the end of the fifteenth century brings to the town its supply of water. From the orchards outside the walls come the sweet green plums for which Elvas is famous. Out of season they can be had preserved in liqueur and coated with icing. The town is equally famous for its dried fruits and olives.

Northeast of Elvas are other citadels which have experienced assaults, sieges and occupation by the enemy. Campo Maior heroically resisted the armies of Spain in the eighteenth century and of France in the Napoleonic era. Portalegre, a much larger town, was originally an outpost of the Roman Empire, like many other towns of the Alentejo. It has ancient aristocratic mansions with carved windows and decorative tiles. The old Augustinian Convent is now the post office; another is the army barracks. Coats of arms of many families are embossed on the flagstones of its cathedral. Farther north is Marvao and Castelo de

Vide, each with old mansions, churches and a castle built for King Dinis late in the thirteenth century. Castelo de Vide is the mecca of artists who come to paint its fifteenth century squares, streets and houses and the views across the valley below it. The town is very busy in midwinter and late summer when countryfolk come to its fairs. Still farther north is the town of Nisa in a mountain region forested with chestnuts, oaks and pines. It is near the gorge of the Tagus and the dam which harnesses the Nisa River for hydroelectric power.

Estremoz, south of these northern citadels, lies along the road over which moves much of the traffic between Portugal and Spain. From the keep of the castle high above its white houses and the ramparts and bastions of its walls, Estremoz looks across groves of silvery-leafed olive trees, vineyards, the dark green of sprawling cork oaks, and the rolling plain. The town is known for the reddish-brown bowls, vases and narrow-necked jugs made by its potters. Figures fashioned from clay of the region are used in nativity scenes throughout the land during the Christmas season.

Many interesting towns crown the isolated hills on the plains around Estremoz. Each September peasants crowd the roads flanked by cork oaks and olive trees that lead to Souzel. It is the time of the fair, one of the major events of this part of the Alentejo. Arraiolos, another medieval walled town, is the home of the carpet-makers whose product, patterned in red and blue, is so popular. Evora-Monte in the Serra da Ossa is rich in history. It not only has a fine thirteenth century castle, but also the house where the Convention of 1834 ending the War of the Two Brothers was signed.

Tourists visit Evora to see the famous cathedral built in the twelfth century, the old city walls, and the Temple of Diana left from the time when the Alentejo was a Roman province. Evora, a major town of this part of Portugal has many reminders of its past under Roman, Goth and Moor. Furniture made by Evora craftsmen is decorated with bright floral patterns on a background of brilliant red or blue.

When Beja was a Roman city it was called Pax Julia. Little is left of either Roman or Moorish times in this town of lower Alentejo.

Other towns of the Alentejo are Alcacer do Sal, Sines, Milfontes and

Vila Vicosa. Alcacer do Sal, once an old Roman town and then a Moorish settlement, is on the River Sado in the western part of the Baixo Alentejo. Around it are rice fields, salt marshes, and huge inverted cones of glistening salt heaped on the banks of the Sado. Sines is in the dune country along the coast. It is the town where Vasco da Gama was born. Milfontes, where fish boats come to moor, is a very old town with relics of the time of the Carthaginians and the Romans. At Vila Vicosa, set in the plains below Estremoz, is the great palace of the dukes of Braganza on the central square. The tombs of the Braganzas are of black and white marble and rest on the backs of carved lions in the church across the square.

The fascination of the Alentejo lies not entirely in its scenery or its historic walled towns. The landscape of the plains is often dull and lonely. But the Alentejanos and their way of life are interesting.

The lot of the peasant has not been an easy one. Men and women wearing black felt hats work in the fields under the hot summer sun. Itinerant laborers help harvest the corn and wheat and beat the ripened olives from the trees. Much of the work on the *quintas* or farms is done by methods we would consider outmoded but they are often better suited to the terrain than more modern methods. On out-of-doors threshing floors burros and oxen are driven in circles over the harvested grain. White cotton-winged windmills perched on a ridge or hill to catch the slightest breeze supply the power to grind the grain between huge boulders.

Moorish influence is seen in this part of the land. Houses with glaring whitewashed walls have chimneys which rise high above the roof and are topped with a lacework of small openings and sometimes adorned with colorful decorations. Water-raising wheels (noras) are quite common throughout the region. Olive trees around some of the towns of the lower Alentejo are said to be descendants of trees planted by the Moors several centuries ago. Fig trees were also brought by Moorish conquerors.

The Alentejano leads a simple life. His food consists of very little meat, except on special occasions, and includes a large proportion of bread and fruits. One of the the most common dishes is called *gaspacho.* It is layers of slices of onions, garlic and cucumbers between slices of bread soaked in oil and vinegar. In some areas pepper-spiced smoked sausage or a stew of goat meat is used. Most of the animals raised on the quintas are sold at local fairs. In the kitchen of the home are large earthenware jars for water, olive oil and other materials used in cooking. The peasant folk wear clothing that is black or some somber color in contrast to the colorful costumes seen in other parts of Portugal. There is little singing or music. Work is fun because many tasks become a game or the basis of a festival. Corn husking is a typical example. All the neighbors are invited to join.

The upper and lower Alentejo are agricultural regions, the major part of it rolling plains where wheat and some corn are grown. Cork, olives, glazed fruits, rice, hogs and sheep are also produced. Winters are quite cold; summers as hot as the summers of central Spain. Shepherds in long cloaks tend the large flocks of merino sheep. Eucalyptus trees have been planted in some parts of the land.

The flatness of parts of the Alentejo can be monotonous. But the little villages glistening white in the distance, the white-walled farmhouses (*montes*) built long and low, the towns on any hill that can be found in the plains and the castle which crowns its summit add charm. The rows of cork oaks that flank the highways and traffic consisting of covered mule carts, ox carts, countryfolk astride little gray burros and the workers in the fields add the touch that gives life to a land that might otherwise be drab and desolate. But, most of all, it is the Alentejano, who at first might seem mournful and melancholy, whose friendliness and smile add the brightness and cheer the Alentejo sometimes lacks.

12 THE ALGARVE

The Algarve, the last of Portugal to be reconquered from the Moors, differs greatly from other regions of the land. Faro, its present capital, was captured in 1249. In the eighth century it had been a Moorish kingdom with the caliph's residence at Silves. There are few remnants of ancient times. Earthquakes and wars have destroyed them. There are the ruins of a Roman spa at Milreu. The largest towns lie on the coastal plain in the southern part of the province between the Serra de Monchique and the Atlantic. Small villages, shimmering white under blue skies, are nestled in valleys. Others fit snugly at the ends of bays poking in from the sea. Hills and valleys are bright with a mosaic of flowers in April and May. Early February brings the pale pink or pearly-white of almond trees in bloom. Cactus clusters grow in the arid soil; squatty fig trees are found in many parts of the province.

The Algarve district is not large. Its total area is slightly less than that of our own state of Delaware. North of the coastal plain are the foothills and ridges of the Serra de Monchique that separate it from the lower Alentejo. In the northeast the Rio Vascao becomes part of the boundary. Spain lies across the Guadiana River to the east. South and west is the Atlantic Ocean.

Moorish influence is quite evident in this part of Portugal. The thick

75

whitewashed walls of the homes shut out summer heat. White chimneys are fretted with a lace-like pattern of holes and vents. Many houses have patios where semitropical plants and small pools and fountains offer a retreat from heat and sunlight. The black scarfs worn over the head on special occasions by the women, the flat roofs and terraces of many Algarve houses, and place names throughout the district are Moorish. Even the name Algarve is derived from the Arab *al-gharb*.

Faro is the largest town and port. In 1596, while Portugal was ruled by Spain, the city was attacked by an English fleet and sacked by its soldiers. It was destroyed again by the great earthquake of 1755. Several ancient churches, the old cathedral, remnants of old houses, and a city gate called the Arch of Rest still stand. Streets have been modernized. The city has become a major Algarve port and a market for figs, bananas, dates and oranges.

Eastward along the coast a few miles from Faro is the town of Olhao with a section of glaring, white, cube-shaped homes. Olhao is not an old town, but the style of these houses gives it more of a Moorish look than many towns that are centuries old. On many a starlit summer evening old Portuguese songs and the music of guitars drift out from narrow streets and terraces on the cool night air. Fishboats bring their catch to Olhao's waterfront. The smell of fish rises from its market place and the large canneries in the town. Some of the fishing craft go far into the Atlantic; many are active in fishing for tuna off the Portuguese coast. The women of Olhao can often be seen in their black-hooded capes on their way to church to pray for their menfolk when storms rage on the open sea.

There are stretches of salt marshes, sand dunes and narrow waterways along the eastern section of the Algarve coast. Many of the towns are unattractive and smell of fish. Near Vila Real de Santo Antonio at the eastern extremity of the southern shore a ferry shuttles traffic across the Guadiana River to Ayamonte on the Spanish side. This Portuguese town is an important market for tuna. It was built by the marquis of Pombal on the site of a town destroyed by a tidal wave during the great earthquake.

Tavira lies to the west. It has some historic old structures with carvings and azulejo decorations. Along the roads to neighboring towns can be seen the horse-drawn carts so common in the region. Bridles are usually decorated with small bells and a spike-like plume. This is a region where cork oaks, grapes, almonds, fig trees and carobs grow. The town of Fuzeta is famous for its wines made from the harvest of local vineyards. Mussels are gathered from rocks in shallow waters offshore.

Many small towns dot the coastal plain in the vicinity of Faro and Olhao. San Bras de Alportel lies in a region where almond trees are abundant and such foods as dried figs with almonds and tasty almond cakes are a specialty. Pork and clams is a popular dish of the region. Loule is a very attractive town because of its elaborate Moorish-style chimneys. Near Albufeira with its glaring white houses are excellent sandy beaches fringing the sea and picturesque grottoes.

A short distance from Portimao, an unattractive fish-canning center on the Algarve coast, is Silves. During the four centuries it was known as Chelb, capital of a Moorish kingdom, it was an important cultural center. The fortress on the hill is peaceful today. Olive trees grow where the armies of King Sancho fought to capture the city late in the twelfth century during the final period of the expulsion of Moslems from Portuguese territory. Silves is an old city. It is believed that centuries ago Phoenician traders formed a settlement on its present site. Today the population is about ten thousand. Cork is the major industry, the bark being obtained from oaks that grow on neighboring hills and plains.

Westward from Portimao is historic Lagos situated on a huge bay capable of harboring a large fleet of ships. From Lagos the caravels in the service of Prince Henry departed on their voyages of discovery. Along the shore of the bay were the shipyards where many of them were built. Slaves brought from Guinea were auctioned under the arches of what is now the customs house of the port. This was the only slave market ever to operate in Portugal.

But the desolate country Prince Henry chose as his paradise lies farther west on the neck of the peninsula that leads to Cape St. Vincent. Here is Sagres overlooking a bay and surrounded by rocky land.

Stunted fig trees, pines and coarse grass cover much of the area where winds from the sea and the thunder of waves plunging against the cliffs add their sounds to the feeling of loneliness. There are the ruins of a fort once used by Prince Henry near the town. Guides also point out slabs of stone in the courtyard which was a compass dial. Only meager remnants of some of the structures built for the prince remain at Vila do Infante. But the view of the cape is the same. Legend has it that this was the spot where the gods came to rest and to watch the sun sink beyond the western horizon, the Sacred Promontory.

The mountains of northern Algarve have few towns. On the ridges of their foothills are the round white windmills like those seen in many parts of Portugal. In their forests are pines, mimosas, chestnut and cork oaks and such an abundance of wild flowers in the spring that it has won for the region the name of "Garden of Portugal." Where these mountains slope into the coastal plain the flora of the north blends with semitropical vegetation. Groves of silvery-leafed olive trees, stands of tall eucalyptus, palms and hundreds of flowering shrubs thrive in its fertile areas.

13 INDUSTRY AND AGRICULTURE

The machine age has brought marked changes to the cities of Portugal in the last twenty-five years. Modern techniques are in use in large factories, canneries and mills where up-to-date laboratories check quality and carry on research in wines, cork products, glass, textiles and cement. Government experiment stations are striving constantly to adapt new plants to Portuguese soil and climate, find new needs for agricultural products, plot strategy in the war on insect and fungus pests.

In many parts of the land the farmer, and the peasant who toils in the field or the forest, still cling to the ways of their forefathers. The small plots of land held by many Portuguese farmers and the nature of the terrain do not permit expensive farm machinery. No attempt is made to upset time-worn practices. Craftsmen often hesitate to discard old ideas. A peasant's life is simple; his needs not difficult to meet.

Centuries-old ways of doing things add to the quaintness of rural life. In the Algarve a mule or an ox tied to a pole plods in endless circles to turn a water wheel. Squat white windmills perch on hilltops or ridges to catch the breeze and grind the farmer's corn. Barefooted country folk join mules, burros and oxen in threshing grain by treading the harvested crop spread outdoors on a rock or cement floor. Although jugs and demijohns are made by the potter in the old-fashioned way, decorative designs are now applied with stencils. Parcels, stacks of cartons, baskets of fish are carried gracefully atop women's heads. In many towns the river bank is the laundry to which housewives flock with the family washing and the anticipation of a chance to chat.

Cork is Portugal's major product. South of the Mondego cork oaks mingle with chestnut trees on the hills, plains and valleys. Laborers skillful in the use of a small double-bitted ax cut into the bark and strip it from the trees. They are the *tiradores*, so essential to the industry.

The cork of commerce is the outer layers of the bark of a certain species of oak that grows so abundantly in Portugal. It is a tissue built of lifeless epidermal cells interspersed with pockets of air. On any hot summer day tiradores are busy in the forests. They cut expertly into the bark without injury to the living cells of the core of the trunk, then peel it away in long strips. Other workers pile the harvest like cordwood to wait until it is taken to the mills.

Only during the heat of summer is stripping permitted and only trees at least twenty years old are stripped. It can be repeated only at nine- or ten-year intervals. The bark obtained from trees less than forty years old cannot be used for making corks or some of the other products of the industry. It is usually ground and, under heat and pressure, used to make cork tile or linoleum. Stripping continues every nine or ten years until the tree is about one hundred and fifty years old.

Protection of the cork oak began many centuries ago during the reign of King Dinis. None can be cut down without permission of government officials. Strict rules must be followed in harvesting the bark. The *Junta Nacional da Cortica,* a commission of the Portuguese government, has authority to enforce regulations aimed toward conservation. Through its efforts new uses of cork have been found. One of these is agglomerated cork in which granules are heated to produce mats and floor coverings. Cork planks are used to make stoppers.

Canned fish is the nation's second most important commercial product. Portuguese fishing fleets have their home ports in nearly a hundred little villages strung along the many miles of Portuguese coast. The olive groves, so plentiful throughout the land, yield the oil not only used for cooking, but also to can the sardines that are exported in enormous quantities. Salt from sea water is harvested on the marshy shore near Aveiro, along the eastern Algarve coast, and in the region south of Lisbon. It is used to salt the vast quantities of codfish caught off the Newfoundland Banks and Greenland.

Cod fishing has been of major importance during Portugal's entire history. A guild of codfish shipowners has existed since early in the sixteenth century. Today broad-beamed, stubby sailing vessels equipped with auxiliary diesel engines and motors to provide lights, heat and refrigeration, travel in spring to the Newfoundland Banks. Each carries a large number of dories on deck. When the fishing grounds are reached these vessels become the mother ships of small fleets of dories. Crew members, one to a dory, venture into fog or rolling seas to trawl by setting long lines with hundreds of dangling hooks. Usually waters not suitable for fishing with drag nets, a method most fishermen of other nations use for harvesting cod, are the areas which the Portuguese choose. When the day is done the catch is cleaned aboard the deck of each mother ship and salted down in her hold. In recent years a supply ship designed and built by Portuguese brings needed provisions, medical and hospital service, and priests to provide religious services. The fleets of the cod fishermen remain in the Newfoundland and Greenland fishing grounds all summer and into early autumn.

The Algarve fishing fleets go far from shore in dangerous seas to search for tuna. Harpooning these huge but very active fish is difficult work requiring great skill. The sardine fleets of Nazare and other west coast towns supply the canneries which pack great quantities for the export trade. Some of the largest fish canneries are at Setubal, Olhao and Faro.

Third in importance commercially is the wine industry. It has flourished in various parts of Portugal since the Romans brought vines to the frontier lands of their empire and Henry of Burgundy brought them to the Douro valley. Each province has vineyards.

One of the most widely known wines is the port which comes from the Douro country and is shipped from Oporto. Since the seventeenth century much of it has gone to England. The Methuen Treaty between England and Portugal, signed in 1703, is responsible for this trade. It not only strengthened military ties between the two countries, but permitted a sharp reduction of duties on port wine entering England. The Portuguese permitted English merchants to sell their textiles freely in Portugal. English wine shippers had been active in Viana do Castelo for many years. Later they formed a large colony in Oporto. The British shippers have their Factory House and their wine lodges at Vila Nova de Gaia across the river from Oporto.

The industry has been greatly improved in recent years. In the Douro valley American vines, immune to parasites which plague many European varieties, are used as the stock on which the Portuguese species are grafted. The wine is stored in the caves of the wine lodges in wooden casks for ageing. The best casks are made from Memel oak obtained from countries along the eastern shore of the Baltic Sea. Chestnut from Portuguese forests is also used. Port is not the only wine obtained from Portuguese vineyards. There are wineries and vineyards in Beira Alta, Madeira, the Algarve and Estremadura producing a great many kinds of wine.

Textile mills and shoe factories have been built. Although woolen cloth and cotton began flowing into Lisbon and Oporto after the signing of the Methuen Treaty, Portugal now supplies much of its needs in its own mills. Today English merchants import considerable quantities of cloth from Portugal. Covilha, with eighty per cent of her employed inhabitants working in her textile mills, is one of the major centers of the industry. Shoes and leather goods are exported to South America and Africa.

The making of fine silver and gold filigree jewelry has flourished for centuries in Oporto and many small towns in northern Portugal. Oporto's goldsmiths and silversmiths amassed large fortunes in the trade. The city is still producing the product.

Other industries have grown in importance in the last few decades. Steel that is imported from Sweden is made into files and these are exported back to Sweden. Coal, sulfur, tungsten, tin and manganese deposits provide minerals and raw materials. The tungsten mines of

Beira Alta province are a source of this valuable metal for making steel and other alloys. Several rivers have been harnessed in mountainous areas where their flow is rapid to produce hydroelectric power. Raw materials for manufactured products are also obtained from overseas colonies. For centuries marble of fine quality has been quarried near Lisbon. Quarries are still producing excellent marble. The cement industry has been expanded. At Marinha Grande in the province of Estremadura the entire population is employed in the glassware industry. Sacavem is a major porcelain center. Embroidery is produced in many small towns, but the most famous embroideries and laces come from the island of Madeira.

Portugal, in the last few decades, has forged ahead. Her increase in the production of materials for export has strengthened her financial condition and stabilized the escudo, the monetary unit of her currency.

14 ART AND ARCHITECTURE

Art has a place in the life of every Portuguese. The altar of the church where he prays, the panels of its nave, the cherubs and angels on the ceiling above him are the work of masters. Goldsmiths and silversmiths have ornamented the organ and fashioned the images glistening in soft rays of flickering candlelight. Much of the work of Portuguese masters is the religious art found in churches, cathedrals and monasteries in all parts of the land. The peasant who strips the bark from the cork oak and the fisherman who mends his nets on the beach at Nazare appreciate color and design. Hearts, flowers linked by curving stems and tendrils, and leaves are embroidered on the linen and cotton many a Portuguese housewife spins. Even the shepherds, to while away lonesome hours with their flocks, carve boxes, mats and spoons from cork and decorate them with colorful patterns. In the simplest homes clusters of flowers fashioned from paper, feathers and carved leather are cherished. In some provinces the furniture is bright with yellow, red and blue blossoms.

This type of art which is so popular is not confined to the home. The peasant who trudges beside huge tawny oxen along the roads of the Douro and Minho country is proud of the wooden yoke they wear. Time, skill and patience have gone into the carving of the crosses and leaves across the breadth of it. The upward-curving prows of fishboats, shaped like the boats of Phoenicians who once traded along Iberian shores, bear the red cross of Christ or the eye of God in bright colors.

The art of the craftsman has changed little over the centuries. Age-old patterns have never gone out of style. Deft fingers that still use cotton, wool or silk floss add beauty to altar cloths, vestments, folk costumes and bed linen. In Minho province chain-stitching is very popular. It was learned from embroidery brought to Portugal by the mariners who first visited ports on the China Sea. Embroidery industries have sprung up in several parts of the land. One is in Castelo Branco, where silk floss is worked into fruit and flower designs and the more complicated motif of the Persian tree of life.

Colored glazed tiles, called azulejos in Portuguese, are used extensively for decoration. They were developed from the geometrically patterned tiles first brought to the Iberian Peninsula by the Arabs. Andalusia was for years the source of Portugal's supply. By the seventeenth century enough were being produced in Lisbon to meet the demand. The scenes depicting historical events, biblical history and legends which are built of azulejos, serve much the same purpose as the fresco paintings on walls in Switzerland, Austria and Bavaria. Some of the finest examples decorate panels, walls and ceilings in shades of rose, yellow, blue or mauve on white. Azulejos on walls indoors or out add the beauty of floral or scenic patterns to public buildings, railroad stations and public gardens in Portugal today. They are as popular now as in the days when artists designed them for Sintra Palace or the gardens of the Palace of the Marques da Fronteira.

In the early years of Portugal's development her kings and members of the nobility were patrons of art. They commissioned artists, sculptors and architects to prepare paintings, sculptures or designs for cathedrals, palaces and monasteries. Life-like reclining figures of deceased kings, queens and princes were made to adorn their tombs. Lace-like ornamentation in stone appeared on monumental structures and statues of marble or bronze graced public squares and gardens. Some of the wealth that came from Brazil and colonies in other newly discovered lands in King Manuel's reign was lavished on such projects. Both

King John and King Alfonso V attracted French, Spanish, Flemish and Italian masters to their courts. Talented young Portuguese developed new techniques.

By the sixteenth century the number of Portuguese artists and architects had greatly increased. It was customary for several individuals to work together on a project in studios in Lisbon, Viseu, Coimbra or Oporto. Because of this practice many a masterpiece of painting bears no signature and art experts find it impossible to determine what artist or artists were responsible for its creation.

The list of Portuguese masters is long. One of the earliest and greatest was Nuno Goncalves who lived in the fifteenth century. His great work, "The Veneration of St. Vincent," was made for the Lisbon cathedral. It shows St. Vincent, the patron saint of Lisbon, receiving the adoration of the royal princes, the clergy, and Portuguese from all walks of life. Included in one of the groups is Prince Henry the Navigator. The painting was made by Goncalves on orders of King Alfonso to commemorate his capture of the Moroccan city of Alcacer.

Other Portuguese artists became famous in later periods. One was Francisco Henriques whose painting, "The Pentecost," is now in the Lisbon Art Gallery. There was John Antunes (1683–1734), who was architect to the court of Pedro II and Francisco de Arruda, architect of the Tower of Belem. Joaquim Machado de Castro (1731–1822), was the sculptor whose fine equestrian statue of King Joseph I graces Black Horse Square in Lisbon. Included among the sixteenth-century artists were Vasco Fernandes, Gregorio Lopez, Cristovao de Figueiredo and Jorge Afonso.

The Arruda family of Evora took an active part over a period of a century in developing some of the great edifices found in Portugal. Miguel de Arruda had a major role during the reign of King John III in the work at Batalha.

Several styles of architecture are seen in the national shrines and monumental buildings. Some are late Gothic, some Romanesque and others Renaissance. Many are mixtures of these and the distinctly Portuguese style born in the Golden Age of discovery while Manuel I was king. It is called Manueline architecture. Pillars take the form of cables, huge jungle vines or tree trunks. Stone is made ornamental by giving it the forms of animals and the blossoms and leaves of exotic plants found in distant lands. It incorporated ideas from the Orient, India and Africa and designs created from the seas on which their caravels sailed, the reefs on which many were wrecked. Navigators of the age of discovery not only returned with material wealth in the form of spices, diamonds, rubies and gold, but also with artistic ideas that were blended to create architectural designs of the Manueline style. There are hundreds of structures throughout Portugal that are striking examples of Manueline and other styles of architecture.

One of the finest buildings is the monastery or abbey of Batalha commemorating the victory over the Castilians on the battlefield of Aljubarrota. Gothic and Manueline styles are blended in this national shrine to Portuguese heroes. It was begun in 1388 long before King Manuel the Fortunate, but work did not cease on it until almost two centuries later. The huge monastery sprawls beside a bend in a road where a little village has sprung up. A town pump where water jugs are filled faces the entrance. Guides take visitors to the high arched nave, the Founder's Chapel with its tombs of King John I and Queen Philippa adorned with recumbent statues of their majesties. A soldier stands on guard by the grave of Portugal's Unknown Soldiers who gave their lives on the battlefields of Flanders and Africa. Swifts dip and soar above the monastery gardens and dart through open windows framed with stone carved in lace-like form.

Along the estuary of the Tagus outside Lisbon are two splendid buildings. One is the Church of the Jeronimos built where Prince Henry the Navigator had constructed a mariners' church as a shrine to Our Lady of Belem. Close by is the Tower of Belem. It was erected after da Gama's discovery of the sea route to India, on the Tagus estuary near the spot where the little fleet of four ships set sail on one of the greatest voyages in world history.

The Church of Christ at Tomar built for the military monastic order of the Templars in the twelfth century is another architectural masterpiece. In its cloister the Spanish king, Philip II, was crowned King Philip I of Portugal at the beginning of that period.

15 PORTUGUESE LITERATURE

Portugal's natural beauty, the charm of village and country life, its festivals and fairs are stimulating to the creative mind. The clouds of lavender that form on Lisbon's hills when jacaranda trees are blooming and the spangles of moonlight where the Mondego skirts historic Coimbra can inspire romantic verses. The battles to defend the nation's independence, desert campaigns against the Moors, and the daring voyages into unknown seas offer a wealth of material for chroniclers, biographers and the creators of tales of adventure. These have brought Portugal a treasury brimming with fine poetry and prose, a literature rich and varied.

Before it became the nucleus of the Portuguese nation, the region of the Douro and northward to the Minho was a part of Galicia. The language was that which a Lusitian people used. It had developed through the absorption of the Latin of Roman conquerors. When Portugal slowly broke away from Galicia its language became a distinct dialect called Galician-Portuguese.

Much of the early literature of Portugal was written or sung in Galician. It consisted of poems handed down from generation to generation; the simple lyrics of the troubadors. Many were never written. They were sung by minstrels. Over the centuries many of them were lost. But in recent times students of literature, working patiently, have unearthed three large collections, a total of more than two thousand poems. Most important of the three is the "Cancioneiro da Ajuda."

Ability to write simple poems was a mark of culture in the twelfth and thirteenth centuries. Learning to write lyrics was part of the education usually given young men of noble birth. The most adept royal poet of the period was King Dinis. He wrote and collected poems and, by providing financial assistance, encouraged others to do the same. In this period thousands of songs were written. Some were love songs. Some were written to accompany the music of folk dances. Others told stories of brave fishermen on stormy seas and lonely shepherds guarding their flocks on the high ridges of Portugal's mountains.

A lapse in writing of lyrics took place shortly after King Dinis died. Ballads then came into style. These were written primarily to accompany folk dances. The Portuguese authors of some of the best used the language of their Spanish neighbors. It seemed better fitted to the style of the ballad than their own.

Lyrics and ballads constituted the type of writing which was most popular in these early times, probably because of the illiteracy of the great mass of the people. These were stories that could be listened to or sung. Prose writing was less common. It was limited to narration or chronicles, to scholarly treatises. There were also some translations into Portuguese of literary masterpieces that had appeared in other lands or were written in ancient times. Some of this writing was done by monks in the seclusion of the monastery. Some came from kings and princes.

Fernando Lopes (1380–1450), was one of the first important masters of prose in Portugal. He had been assigned the task of writing the chronicles of the reigns of Portugal's first ten kings. Years of research by travel throughout the kingdom and delving into the dusty documents stored in the royal archives were a part of his task. All that remains of the work today are the chronicles of the reigns of Fernando, John I, and Pedro.

Father John Alvares wrote the story of the very dramatic events in the life of Prince Fernando. This was the brother of Prince Henry who voluntarily became a hostage of the Moors and martyr rather than return the city of Ceuta to the infidels.

Portugal was making history at a rapid rate in the sixteenth century. Historians were kept busy writing the chronicles of that adventurous Golden Age. Discovery of new lands and new routes to reach the Orient provided a wealth of material. It was an age in which men of talent sought to attach themselves in some way to the royal court to win financial aid.

Gil Vicente (about 1465–1536), came to the court in Lisbon early in his life. He was the son of a goldsmith who lived in Guimaraes. He had talent both in his father's craft and in writing. Religious poems had constituted his early literary interests. The young poet, while working as a goldsmith, used every effort to bring his poetry to the attention of the queen. He succeeded on many an occasion. It won him the assignment of writing plays for court celebrations and special events. They brought fame to Gil Vicente. His more than forty plays were used in performances for the entertainment of the court. They earned him the title of "father of the Portuguese theater."

Many historians wrote extensively during this period. Some were chroniclers attached to the court who had access to reports and records. Others were adventurous men who went on their own to see the fabulous new worlds Portuguese navigators had discovered and to bring back the story. One of the most famous of these was the historian Joao de Barros (1496–1570). Barros came originally from the Minho country of northern Portugal. He lived as a boy in Lisbon. Although he held a minor government position, his life was devoted to writing. He launched a stupendous project in which he planned a many-volumed history of the great discoveries of the Portuguese. His work entitled *Asia* was based on government records to which he had access. He toiled ceaselessly in its preparation. The immensity of the task prevented its completion before his death, but other volumes were added by Diogo do Couto, who continued the work.

Other writers were traveling to the Portuguese possessions and beyond to gather material. Gomes Eanes de Zurara wrote about Guinea and the work of Prince Henry the Navigator. Fernao Mendes Pinto traveled throughout the Orient to produce his *Peregrination*. Benito de Gois, who became a Jesuit priest, wrote a journal while he traveled through central China.

Greatest of all Portuguese men of literature was Luis de Camoes (1524–1580). He is known to the English-speaking world as Camoens. There are many details of his life that are not definite. He was poor. His family belonged to one of the lower orders of the nobility. Indirectly he was related to Vasco da Gama. Camoens' life was packed with heartbreaks and misfortune, but brimming with adventure. Out of it came a manuscript, written over a period of many years, published under the title *Os Lusiadas* (*The Lusiads*). It is Portugal's national poem, its great epic.

After Camoens had studied Latin and the classics at the University of Coimbra he went to Lisbon. His lyrics and sonnets probably attracted some attention. The splendor of court functions, the coming and going of vassal monarchs from possessions overseas, and the pomp of ceremonies made less of an impression than did a lady-in-waiting in the retinue of the queen. Camoens fell in love. The romance came to the attention of the king and the young writer was banished from Lisbon. He spent the next few years as a soldier in northern Africa and had the misfortune of losing the sight in his right eye.

Life in Lisbon, the most dazzling capital of Europe at the time, was irresistible to Camoens. He returned. Poverty and the habit of getting into difficulties returned with him. Two years of life in Lisbon came to an end when he struck an officer of the royal court with his sword and wounded him. The incident occurred in a crowded street during the Corpus Christi celebrations. It brought him a prison sentence.

In the life of Camoens penalties such as banishment and prison terms seemed to be merely the prelude to more serious difficulties. Through the efforts of influential friends he received a pardon from the king after serving less than a year of his long term. But the pardon was granted upon condition that he do military service in India.

He arrived in Goa, capital of the Portuguese possessions in the Far East, in 1553. His poetry attracted the attention of the viceroy. To assist him, this official sent him to Macao, a Portuguese possession near what is now Hong Kong. He was to fill a minor government position. Two years ended his stay in Macao. He was arrested for infringement of certain regulations and put in chains aboard a ship bound for Goa. Misfortune traveled with him. The vessel was wrecked near the mouth of a river in the South China Sea and the only possessions Camoens was able to save were the several cantos of *The Lusiads* he had completed. Another prison term, another pardon obtained through the request of a viceroy who was his friend, and he was on his way back to Lisbon. Although the long journey home started in 1567, misfortune, lack of funds and sickness prevented him from reaching Lisbon until three years later. At times his only valuable possession was the precious manuscript, tattered and soiled, that he had been writing during his days in prison, aboard ship and in the far corners of the Orient. Fortunately when he reached his destination the official of the Inquisition whose duty it was to pass on all manuscripts before granting permission for publication was lenient. The poem was published in 1572.

The Lusiads tells the story of Vasco da Gama's voyage and the events of the age of discovery. Other happenings in Portuguese history are also included. Worked through the poem are references to the Greek gods, an artifice that gives it an unusual turn. Some critics feel this detracts from the story; others, that it enhances it.

The last years of Camoens' life were uneventful. A meager pension was granted him by young King Sebastian. Upon his death in 1580, there was no special burial. Not until three centuries later what was believed to be the great poet's remains were entombed in the church at Belem.

When Portugal's Golden Age had come to an end there was a marked decrease in the production of books. Literary work had been financed or sponsored usually by grants from the king or the benevolence of wealthy members of the nobility. The slump in the nation's economy meant less financial aid to poets and prose writers. Books were very expensive. A large segment of the nation was illiterate. Despite these conditions, outstanding work was produced, but not in as great a volume as in previous decades.

In 1735 a collection of eyewitness accounts of some of the maritime disasters involving Portuguese ships in the latter part of the sixteenth century was published. It was called the *Historia Tragico-Maritima*. Alexandre Herculano (1810–1877), began a very scholarly *History of Portugal*. The criticism of his treatment of some events in the story, particularly by members of the clergy, was disheartening to the author. So great was his disappointment at the reception it received he dropped the idea of continuing the work after only the first four of the volumes had been completed. So great was his anger at the clergy that he wrote and had published the story of the Inquisition.

There was a slowly increasing number of poets and prose writers making contributions to Portuguese literature in the nineteenth and twentieth centuries. The historical novel came into vogue. Poems about the life of the peasant, the history of the nation, and about various regions of the land were published. Aquilino Ribeiro chose as the locale for his novels a part of Beira Alta. Others chose the Minho, the Algarve, and the Alentejo. Out of the efforts of its poets, dramatists, historians, and novelists has developed a literature surpassing in richness and number of works the literature of many much larger nations.

16   FESTIVALS, FAIRS AND HOLIDAYS

The Portuguese calendar is brimming with fairs and festivals. These colorful celebrations attract countryfolk from miles around. They come to town in carts brightly painted and bedecked with blossoms. Everyone is ready to join in the fun of folk dances, singing, battles of flowers and parades. Each looks forward to the color and thrills of the *festa brava* (the bullfight) and the wonderful fireworks display. There are pilgrimages on holy days to little white chapels perched on a mountain or clinging to rugged cliffs overlooking the sea. Precious statues are borne in solemn procession under canopies of purple velvet embroidered with silver or gold along streets strewn with rose petals. There are the ceremonies of blessing the fishing fleet before it sails out to sea and the outdoor Mass for the *campinos* in colorful garb before the opening of the bullfight season in Vila Franca de Xira. During the Festival of the Green Cap on the second Sunday in August the salt pans of Alcochete in Estremadura are blessed. In the *Festa dos Tabuleiros* maidens dressed in white parade down Tomar's streets. On their heads they carry large wicker baskets decorated with flowers and filled with loaves of bread and sausages. When the parade is over the loaves are distributed among the poor. Portugal is a land with a warm, sunny climate where flowers bloom all year and conditions are ideal for merrymaking.

Holy days which have become national, regional or local holidays are not the only occasions for celebrations. The change of season, the anniversary of great historic events and holidays like Christmas and the New Year are also red-letter days. Carnival is a period marked with gaiety. Restoration Day, commemorating the overthrow of sixty years of Spanish rule, is a patriotic national day. It is celebrated on December the first and is usually centered about *Mocidade Portuguesa,* a kind of militia formed by students. These youths in green shirts and dark yellow trousers parade down city streets. The day is also marked by patriotic speeches and religious services.

Coimbra, in late May, becomes the setting of a fascinating facet of student life. This quaint old city, with its university founded in the thirteenth century, witnesses many traditional customs. Student republics still exist. These are the dormitories with mess halls regulated according to ancient rules enforced by upper classmen. Coimbra's undergraduates wear the distinctive black costume, white shirt and, in appropriate weather, a long symbolic black cape. Juniors and seniors wear on their briefcases the ribbons which denote by color their field of study. Red indicates law; yellow, medicine; violet, pharmacy. During the festivities of *Queima das Fitas* marking the end of the school year the ribbons are burned in a great bonfire. Freshmen, in traditional ceremonies, receive the passes that end the restrictions governing their first year. The festival is also marked by processions and a magnificent ball.

Down in the Tagus valley not far from Lisbon are the pastures where bulls are raised for the bullfights. This is in the Ribatejo country. At Vila Franca de Xira, one of the largest towns of the region, the colorful festival of the Red Waistcoat is held during the full of the moon in July. The big celebration is in honor of the campino and marks the opening of the bullfight season in Vila Franca de Xira. These Portuguese cowboys wear their colorful costume. It consists of a green stocking cap bordered with red, dark knee breeches, white shirt, bright red waistcoat and linen stockings. The starched shirt collar is fastened with two pairs of miniature gold filigree bells and both shirt and stockings are embroidered. The waistcoat is trimmed with glass buttons. The cowboys assemble in the square of the town astride their fast horses and carrying the *pampilho*. This is a long wooden pole with a sharp metal tip with which they guide or urge the black bulls from pasture to the bull ring. Each rider wears a metal badge with the landowner's family crest.

Vila Franca de Xira is decorated for the festival. Embroidered bedspreads and draperies are hung from windows and flowers and flags add color. Shop windows have appropriate displays. Late on Saturday afternoon the mayor presents the oldest campino with a new pampilho in a ceremony before the town hall. Crowds surge into the streets leading from the bridge which spans the Tagus. Over this route campinos bring a number of bulls into the town. They are turned loose in barricaded streets for the fun that follows. It is an opportunity for any amateur bullfighters from the crowds who are daring enough to try their skill. The bulls are then returned to their pastures and the townsfolk enjoy an evening of dancing and singing. Under the moon an open-air Mass is held with a procession of the candles and campinos on horseback encircling the altar. The bulls are brought back for more street skirmishes on Sunday and then to the bull ring. The bullfight in late afternoon is the climax of the festival.

Many Portuguese towns have bull rings where bullfights are held on Sundays or holidays. The seasons vary. Usually they occur during the months of May to November. The Portuguese know them as festa brava or a *tourada*. They are markedly different from the bullfights of Spain. With bands playing and the stands crowded with enthusiastic spectators, the spectacle begins with the *cortesias* or parade into the ring of all who take part. The bullfighters on horseback (the *cavaleiros*) wear long silk or velvet jackets of brilliant colors embroidered with silver or gold, black riding boots, and feathered three-cornered cocked hats. The *bandarilheiros* and *matadors* fight the bull on foot. The animal's horns have been carefully padded to prevent injury to the horses. The matador, forbidden by Portuguese law to kill the bull, must merely simulate the act.

Religious ceremonies of some kind are usually a part of any fair or festival. Portugal is a Catholic country. Even the smallest town has its church as the center of saint's day ceremonies or the start of a pilgrimage *(romaria)*. Small town churches are quite simple and often lack the lavish interior decoration of those of large cities. The walls are whitewashed. The deep-toned bells in the belfry call the faithful to Mass. The altar is adorned with blue and white azulejos. Flowers are always in evidence. The candles with garlands of tinted or gold flowers carved in wax are created by craftsmen.

Pilgrimages are common throughout the land. The pilgrimages to the Shrine of Our Lady of Fatima attract thousands. Many have also become the occasion for a fair. There is a weekly fair at Barcelos in northern Portugal where regional pottery is featured among the commodities of all kinds that are on sale. The *Feira dos Pucarinhos* in February at Evora also features pottery. The March fair of St. Bento at Santo Tirso is noted for displays of earthenware, including miniatures, dolls, animals and small statues and usually lasts for weeks. Hundreds of festivals, fairs and pilgrimages are held during the year.

Christmas is Portugal's most important holiday. It is a family celebration, a *Festa da Familia*. Flowers are in bloom, except in the extreme northeast where high altitudes and cold winds bring snow. Housewives make extra preparations for the season of festivities. The home is cleaned. A Nativity scene, a Christmas tree, or both are set up in either the living or dining room. Since Portugal is a Catholic country, the Nativity scene is usually the center of the decorative scheme. In most cases the Christmas tree is a small pine. There is the custom of exchanging presents that is a part of Christmas in other Christian lands.

At eleven o'clock on Christmas Eve members of the family gather for supper. Boiled codfish and potatoes are the traditional dish. It is served with a sweet rice pudding and probably *rabanadas,* a dish made by dipping slices of bread in an egg sauce, frying, and simmering the fried slices in a sugar sauce. Sometimes *mechidos,* a kind of pudding made from dried fruits, is a part of this Christmas Eve supper. The dishes served vary in different parts of the land.

At midnight everyone attends Mass in the village church. When Mass is over, the family returns home for cakes, cold meats and dried fruits. In some homes this is the time for distributing gifts. In others, each boy or girl leaves a shoe near the chimney, the Christmas tree, or the Nativity scene. Next morning they wake up early and rush to see what presents have been left in their shoes. In most Portuguese homes it is said that *Menino Jesus* (the Christ Child) sends the gifts and, in some, that Father Christmas delivers them. The traditional Christmas Day dish is turkey or, with families which cannot afford it, chicken.

King's cake is eaten sometime during the period from Christmas to January sixth. It is a round cake made mostly of glazed fruit and baked in it are one or two gifts and a large bean. When it is sliced and served the one unfortunate enough to get the bean must buy the cake the next year.

New Year's Eve is celebrated much the same as in other lands. Noise-making, the ringing of church bells, beating of drums and blaring of trumpets announce the approach of the new year. In many towns the night sky is made brilliant with fireworks. The celebration and fireworks that welcomes the new year at Funchal, Madeira, is one of the most widely known celebrations of its kind.

There are traditional delicacies for Easter Sunday. One is almonds coated with a colored sugar icing. The other is a sweet cake decorated with hard-boiled eggs.

The patron saint of each town is honored by a local celebration on the appropriate day. In Oporto it is St. John's Day, late in June. At night the streets and squares in the heart of the city are closed to traffic so that there can be dancing and singing without interruption. December the eighth is a national holiday honoring Our Lady of the Conception *(Senhora da Conceicao)*, the protector of the nation. In recent years it has also become the Portuguese Mother's Day *(Dia da Mai)*. Portuguese boys and girls show their love for their mother on this day, present her with gifts and a special cake is made for the occasion.

Sunshine, an abundance of flowers, and the natural beauty of the Portuguese countryside provide a perfect setting for any holiday.

Whether the event is a romaria in the north, one of the great fairs in the towns of the Alentejo, a feast day or a bullfight, there is always rejoicing. What pleasure and pride come to the Portuguese girl on festival days when she can don all the finery of silks, embroidery and gold or silver filigree that comprises the folk costume worn by her people for many generations! At the great fair held in front of the castle at Guimaraes there will be merriment and the music of the calliope. Torchlight parades will brighten the narrow streets of Lisbon during the feast of St. Anthony. There will be the famous battle of flowers at Loule in the Algarve during Twelfth Night celebrations. Holidays all over Portugal are happy days.

17 THE BEIRA COUNTRY

The Beiras, three provinces of central Portugal, stretch southward from the Douro valley until they reach the borders of the provinces of Estremadura, Ribatejo and Alentejo. One is the coastal area called Beira Litoral. The other two, dividing the region of mountain ranges, are Beira Baixa and Alta. The rugged peaks of the Serra da Estrela, snow-clad in winter, reach from the Spanish border southwestward to the Tagus. In this mountain country is the source of the Mondego, the largest river lying entirely within Portugal. In each of the three provinces quaint customs are preserved and ancient structures are vivid reminders of the historic past of the nation.

At the northern end of the Beira coast is the great lagoon, the Ria de Aveiro, reaching from the sea. Bordering its shore are salt marshes, sand dunes and pasture lands, reclaimed like the polders of Holland, where cattle graze. A long arm of dunes lies between it and the open Atlantic. Seaweed, which is used as fertilizer, salt and several varieties of fish are taken from the waters of the *ria* (lagoon). Oxen tow rakes to dig the vegetation from its floor. Men with forks and rakes wade knee-deep in its shallows to gather seaweed. Along the fringes of the ria are the flats, checkered with mud-walled squares which are the salt pans where sea water is imprisoned to evaporate in the sun. The salt that is left is gathered in baskets and dumped in cone-shaped piles which look like glistening white pyramids at a distance.

Aveiro, a town with about eighteen thousand inhabitants, is the largest on the north Beira coast. It is built on the edge of the lagoon. Canals which cut through its business district link it with both the lagoon and the ocean. Where the wide Central Canal, busy with fishing boats and salt barges, joins the Canal of the Pyramids there is the Rossio, the town square. Each March it is the site of Aveiro's month-long fair with music, dancing and the awarding of prizes to seaweed-carrying boats that have the most beautiful prows. Throughout the town are several historic churches with a wealth of art treasures of the fifteenth and sixteenth centuries.

The boats of the seaweed-gatherers and the fishermen have up-turned prows decorated with brightly colored designs. In shape they have a slight resemblance to the gondolas of Venice. Historians tell us their form is similar to that of the boats of the Phoenicians who settled on this part of the Iberian coast some two thousand years ago. The people of the province are probably descendants of these early settlers because they also have strikingly Phoenician-like characteristics.

The fishing, seaweed-gathering, and salt industries create much of the activity in Aveiro. Boats laden with baskets of eels, skate, mullet, clams and sardines from the open sea, come to its quays by way of the network of canals. These industries sustain the town's inhabitants. A most popular dish is *caldeirada a pescadora,* a thick soup or chowder made from eels, fish, clams and potatoes. In the shops little wooden tubs of preserved eels and eggs can be purchased.

The largest city of the Beira coastal area is Coimbra. It is also Portugal's third largest city. Where it rises on the banks of the Mondego River, there was once a city of the Romans. It was captured when the Moors invaded the Iberian Peninsula. When it was recovered by the Christians it became the Portuguese capital until, in the thirteenth century, Lisbon was given that distinction. A university, founded in 1290, remained in Coimbra permanently after it was returned from Lisbon by King John III in 1537. The old cathedral and the Augustinian monastery, both built by Alfonso Henriques, and the ancient church and convent of Santa Clara are just a few of the historic structures in this great Portuguese cultural center. The statue and silver tomb of Queen St. Isabel, wife of King Dinis, whose loaves of bread given to the poor are said to have changed to roses, have been moved from the Santa Clara church. The structure was gradually sinking in the water and sands along the banks of the Mondego. Coimbra is rich in sculpture, paintings and masterpieces of the craft of the goldsmith.

Coimbra has become famous because of its university, second oldest in Europe. From a considerable distance can be seen its bell tower on the hill overlooking the Mondego. The university lies in what is called the Upper Town. Among the older buildings there is the lavish library built by King John V with its many thousands of volumes and precious manuscripts. Most of the old rooming houses which housed the traditional student republics have been torn down and replaced by the modern structures of the new University City. Coimbra's students still cling to old customs. Some are traditions centuries old, like the wearing of long black capes, the rules that govern the conduct of underclassmen, and those regarding graduation exercises and studies.

Coimbra also has a beautiful botanical garden and one of the most unique children's parks in Europe. Little Portugal has child-size houses representing all the types of domestic architecture found in the land. In a separate section are replicas of gardens and palaces of each of the colonies with appropriate displays. A children's restaurant and zoo are included.

Shrines, historic cities and fishing villages extend the length of the province. Peat bogs, dunes, olive groves, and forests of pine and eucalyptus give variety to the landscape. In the picturesque town of Leiria a fine old medieval castle built by Alfonso Henriques stands atop a hill. In the thirteenth century it became a favorite residence of King Dinis and Queen St. Isabel. The pines which Dinis had planted to keep the sand dunes from working inland from the coast have been carefully protected. They form the Leiria State Forest.

On the thirteenth of each month, between May and October, the roads leading to the little village of Fatima in the southern part of the Beira country are crowded. Pilgrims from all parts of Portugal come by burro, ox or mule cart, horse-drawn carriages, automobile, bus or train. They come to visit the Shrine of Our Lady of Fatima. It was here on the dry, sparsely wooded plateau south of Leiria that on May 13, 1917, an image of the Virgin Mary appeared to three little children who were tending a flock of sheep. An impressive basilica has been erected here, facing a huge square where pilgrims to the shrine kneel in prayer.

Figueira da Foz, where the Mondego River empties into the Atlantic, is one of Portugal's most popular seashore resorts. It is also the home port of many of the vessels of the cod-fishing fleet. Racks where cod dries in the sun can be seen at the little villages near this fashionable resort.

Moving inland from the rice fields, salt pans and fishing villages of the Beira coast, roads lead higher and higher as they approach the Spanish border. This is the rugged mountainous part of the Beira country. There are forests of chestnut and oak, pine and fir, and barren stretches strewn with mammoth boulders, black and forbidding.

The northern fringe of Beira Alta, where it skirts the Douro River, is lonely mountain country. Towns are great distances apart. Castles built centuries ago to stem any invasion tide across the border from Spain still crown some of its rugged peaks. There are rock deposits rich in tungsten. Shepherds guard their flocks seeking sparse vegetation on lonely slopes. The countryfolk toil with primitive tools. In many a mountain home which is little more than a shelter against storms and winter cold, wool is spun and made into the coarse handwoven blankets for which the region is famous.

Guarda, the highest town in Portugal, lies just off the main highway crossing the border and leading into Spain. The hill on which it is built looms above the boulder-strewn plain. This fortress town was founded by King Sancho I in 1199. Caesar with his invading army halted near the site long before the town was built. There are arched stone gates along its narrow streets and an imposing cathedral built entirely of granite.

Near Guarda are the ridges and deep valleys of the Serra da Estrela, a range possessing all the scenic beauty of the Swiss Alps. Giant granite monoliths give part of the area a strange and weird appearance. There are splendid examples of dolmens, the prehistoric burial tombs built of great rock slabs.

Viseu, west of Guarda, is the capital of the old province of Beira Alta. Its houses and the small palaces where members of the nobility once lived are made of granite. The great cathedral dates from the twelfth century. Since Viseu is the center of a large agricultural region it holds a celebration lasting many days in autumn called the Fair of St. Mateus. Products are brought by mule and ox-cart or on the backs of burros from all parts of Beira Alta. Cattle, fruit, cheese and corn are sold in the market. Baskets, lace, wickerwork from Vila de Moinhos and the black earthenware pottery that shines like pewter from Molelos are offered to interested customers by the peasant folk who have created them.

There is interesting country in the vicinity of Viseu. In June the people of Vila de Moinhos enjoy the Festival of St. John. A special feature is the *cavalhades*. This is a riding contest that has been held for the last three centuries. The horseback riders wear a costume that consists of a white tunic, a crown of carnations on the head, and a green stick in the hand. Not far from Viseu is the Cave of Viriatus, the Lusitanian hero who so successfully routed the Roman armies on more than one occasion. Viriatus is said to have been born in the mountain fastnesses of one of the ranges of the Serra da Estrela.

Castelo Branco is the largest city in Beira Baixa. It has grown around the old walled town that was a stronghold of the Templars, one of the military monastic orders which in early times established forts in Portugal's frontier country. It has the old bishop's palace with its beautiful formal gardens.

A number of years ago a contest was held to determine the "most Portuguese village in Portugal." Monsanto, in Beira Baixa, was the winner. A silver rooster high atop one of the towers of the town denotes this distinction. Much of the old fortifications remain with many other reminders of the battles and sieges that have marked its history.

A few other important towns of the province are Covilha, Fundao and Belmonte. Covilha is the gateway to the ski country in the Serra da Estrela.

The whole mountain-ribbed interior of the Beira country is a land that is sometimes wild and desolate, with villages far apart. It is the homeland of a patriotic people who still cling to old ways and costumes. Along the winding high roads are crude shelters of granite slabs where shepherds or travelers can find protection from torrential rains or howling winds. Flocks of sheep roam through wilderness country attended by shepherds in long heavy woolen or straw capes. Old fortified towns or little clusters of granite houses appear on rock-studded slopes. Olive trees grow in some of the valleys. In summer, heather blooms on barren mountainsides and plateaus. It is a land famed for fine wines, blankets of hand-woven wool, and pottery; a part of Portugal that has remained almost unchanged since hordes of invaders from the east and south fought to scale its castle walls.

18 ESTREMADURA AND RIBATEJO

The provinces of Estremadura and Ribatejo lie south of the Beiras. Together they form one of the most fascinating parts of Portugal. The region reaches into the valley of the Tagus where the black bulls and fast horses are raised for the bull ring. On its northern edge is the architectural gem of the monastery of Batalha, built to fulfill the vows of a king who prayed for victory on the eve of battle. Where it touches the sea there are fishing villages. When the young bulls are being branded on the ranches near Vila Franca de Xira, the sun is drying the long black nets spread on the sand at Nazare, Portugal's most typical fishing village.

In the paradise that is Sintra ancient castles crown forested hilltops and flower clusters hang like colored foam from the stone walls flanking village streets. Up the Tagus, in the Ribatejo, a thirteenth-century castle still stands on its island in the middle of the stream. In many an Estremadura town freshly made pottery is set out to dry in the sun. It is a region where pilgrimages to the shrine of a patron saint become a joyous festival or even a picnic. It completely surrounds Lisbon. Carts and trucks loaded with beans, fish, corn and wine bring these products to Lisbon's markets. The economy and life of the entire area is keyed to the needs of the capital city.

A road branching from the Lisbon-Oporto highway leads to Nazare in northern Estremadura. The town has no castle or monastery. Compared with other Portuguese towns, it is relatively young. There are two distinct parts, the *praia* (beach) and the *sitio* (hill). First sight of the praia reveals a wide strip of houses gleaming white against the background of the blue Atlantic. This is where the fisherfolk live. Tall, cubical houses, somewhat Moorish in style, flank lanes little more than six feet wide. From clotheslines strung from upper windows, washings catch both the sunlight and the breeze from the sea. A wide thoroughfare skirts the beach, the place where the people of Nazare work and play.

The dress of the people, the way they work and the fishboats make Nazare's praia a colorful place to see. Everyone goes barefoot. Many of the women and girls wear a pot-shaped black felt hat and a dress and cape that is also black. The dresses flare out with the seven pleated petticoats worn under them. Some women sit all day at the edge of the beach, gaze at the sea and mourn their menfolk who have met death in its storms. The Atlantic takes a heavy toll each year.

The costume of the Nazare fisherman is more colorful than the dress of its women. The loose checkered woolen shirt and trousers are almost as bright as the tartans of Scotland. On the head is a long black stocking cap hung to partially shade the face from the sun.

When a fishboat rides shoreward on the crests of waves from the open sea, a team of oxen usually is waiting to pull it up on the beach. The boats do not have the sharply up-turned prow of the boats of Aveiro, but all are adorned with some brightly colored design such as the eye of God, flowers, or the cross of Christ. Nazare boats are broad of beam to fit them for riding the heavy ground swells and turbulent seas offshore. Some are propelled with oars; others, by sails and diesel engines. Strung against their masts are lamps of unusual shape designed to cast a beam or spot of light on the water during night fishing. The light attracts fish toward the nets.

The beach is the place where most of the activity of this fishing village occurs. The old men sit within the pattern of the nets sprawled on the sand for hundreds of feet. Each is busy mending or making other repairs. White pigskin water bags dangle from poles stuck in the sand looking like carcasses bloated in the heat of the sun. Girls with big earthenware jugs congregate at the village pump. When the jugs are filled they carry them home atop their head, a duty that seems to have fallen entirely to Portuguese women. When a boat arrives with its harvest from the sea, barefooted fishwives line up with their big shallow baskets and wait their turn. Then, with baskets loaded with fish and placed atop the head, they race the long stretch to the market place to be among the first to offer them for sale.

There is a chapel in the upper town called the Chapel of Our Lady of Nazare. Legend has it that a Portuguese nobleman riding in pursuit of a deer in the fog was saved from death by a miracle. When his horse had reached the brink of the precipice where the face of the cliff slopes into the sea, the Virgin Mary appeared, turned the animal about and thus saved the nobleman's life. For ten days in September the people of Nazare hold festivities in honor of the patron saint. There are pilgrimages to this shrine on the cliff's edge, a fair, colorful dancing of the fandango on the walk that faces the sea and all the fireworks and fanfare so important in a gay Portuguese festival.

North from Nazare is Batalha or, the monastery of Our Lady of Victory. The little town beside this great national shrine is of no major importance. It has a pension where travelers can stop for the night, a cobbler's shop and several shops where the earthenware of Estremadura can be purchased. The monastery, begun by King John I in 1388, stands in the valley. On the eve of the battle of Aljubarrota, King John prayed for victory and promised that if his prayers were answered he would build an abbey near the spot. The battle between the small Portuguese force supported by English crossbowmen, under command of Nuno Alvares, met and defeated an overwhelming armored force of Castilians. The decisive victory led to withdrawal of the enemy from King John's realm. The main part of the abbey, one of the finest examples of Gothic architecture in Europe, was completed in 1433. For more than a hundred years after its completion additions were made by Edward, Alfonso V and Manuel I.

Another large monastery is a short distance from Batalha. It is the monastery of Alcobaca. Historians say it was built by Alfonso Henriques because of a vow he made before wresting from the Moors the stronghold of Santarem in the Ribatejo. The abbey and much of the surrounding territory was given to Cistercian friars who did much to colonize and convert to agricultural use lands ravished in the wars with the Moors. Architects from Burgundy were brought into the country to plan the abbey.

There are many picturesque towns and an abundance of natural beauty in northern Estremadura. Peniche is a small fishing port where the ocean is whipped to froth on the rocky coast. Just a couple of miles offshore are the Berlengas, a group of small islands. A monastery for the monks of the Order of St. Jerome and, at a later date, a fortress was built on one of them. Inland from Peniche is the medieval town of Obidos with a castle that has been standing since the wars with the Moors. The little white-walled town with narrow stone-paved streets also commands a splendid view over the surrounding country. Farther south, at Mafra, is the huge monastery built by King John V. It was completed in 1717. The convent has more than eight hundred rooms. It was once used as a royal residence.

Torres Vedras is a town in an important wine-producing district not far north of Lisbon. Since the capital city is an excellent market for vegetables, the peasants living near Torres Vedras work small plots to supply this need.

There are more resort towns and fishing villages along the Estremadura coast south of Lisbon. The largest is Setubal near the mouth of the Sado River. Great numbers of fishing boats make it their home port. In the city are the largest sardine canneries in Portugal. In the salt pans of the marshy areas along the river large quantities of salt are harvested. Setubal is an old city and lies within a short distance of excellent beaches on the peninsula.

To the east, wedged between the provinces of Estremadura and Alto Alentejo, is the Ribatejo. Santarem, on the north bank of the Tagus, is the provincial capital. The most interesting part of this city is astride the hill that overlooks the river. It was a Roman stronghold centuries ago. In the eighth century it fell to the Moors and five hundred years later was taken by the Christians. Some of its most historic structures have been destroyed. One that remains was once the Jesuit college. It has many old corridors adorned with excellent azulejos.

Tomar, in the northern part of the province, was a city of the Knights Templars. During the reign of King Dinis it became the headquarters of the Order of Christ which the king had organized to replace the Templars. The great monastery or Convent of Christ is its outstanding structure.

Grapes are grown in many parts of the Ribatejo for the wineries and there are extensive groves of olive trees. Near Vila Franca de Xira bulls and horses are raised. It is the region of the campino.

19 MADEIRA AND THE AZORES

Far out in the Atlantic are two groups of Portuguese islands. Each group has the status of a province, not a colony. The Madeiras, almost six hundred miles from Lisbon, lie off the northwest coast of Africa. About nine hundred miles due west of Lisbon are the Azores. It is believed that both were visited at some early time by the Phoenicians and, later, the Genoese. No settlements were made and none were inhabited. During the reign of King Dinis navigators sailed westward and touched at one of the islands of the Azores. Not until the time of Prince Henry was any attempt made to colonize them. Madeira, completely forgotten, was rediscovered by two of Prince Henry's mariners, Joao Goncalves Zarco and Tristao Vaz Teixeira, in 1419. Ancient atlases and charts brought to Sagres had shown their approximate location. The prince's men brought back glowing tales of their beauty and climate. Colonists were sent the following year. Soon vegetation from Mediterranean lands was introduced. Over the centuries these plants developed and spread to add new beauty to valleys and mountainsides.

There are five islands in the Madeiras. The largest bears the name of the group. The others are Porto Santo and a chain of three smaller islands known collectively as the Desertas. Madeira, the island on which the capital, Funchal, is located, is the top of a submerged mountain range. Pico Ruivo rises more than six thousand feet above sea level. The range extends the length of the island which is thirty miles. It is marked by great lateral ridges separated by deep valleys. Near the island the ocean floor is eight to ten thousand feet below the surface. Madeira has an area of 285 square miles and a population of about a quarter of a million people.

Visitors who come to Madeira to enjoy the mild climate, flowers, fruits and hospitality of the islanders usually arrive by seaplane or ship at the charming city of Funchal. There are many thousands of visitors each year. Funchal is a port of call for ships from many parts of the world. It lies on the major sea lanes linking Europe, Africa and South America.

Funchal, largest city in this island paradise, is set in an amphitheater of green mountains and built around a curving shore. It has a population of almost one hundred thousand. White-walled houses, the splashes of red and magenta of clusters of blossoms where bougainvillaea vines sprawl across roof tiles, and the fronds of palms make it a colorful city. Jacarandas, native to Brazil and as big as oak trees, line many of its streets. Nature's finest display comes when, before leaf buds have opened wide, their branches become masses of pale blue or lavender blossoms.

Passengers from ships and planes land at the *cais* (quay) which pokes into the blue-green waters of the harbor and then go to the wide Avenida do Mar skirting the sea. They are met by vendors carrying baskets bulging with flowers of every color. Other vendors offer wickerwork novelties or flowers made from the feathers of birds of the island. Some passengers rest for a while in the shade of trees with leaves hidden by masses of blossoms flaming red or brilliant yellow. Others seek transportation to their hotels beyond the heart of the city.

Most visitors new to Funchal shun the taxis. They choose to ride in bullock sledges with cretonne curtains and mounted on steel runners. These sledges are drawn by oxen over the shiny cobblestones of the city's streets. Some take a bullock sledge to the Monte, a district about two thousand feet above the harbor and five miles from the heart of town. Then, for the thrill of a lifetime, they make the return trip in a wickerwork toboggan guided by Madeiran drivers and slide all the way on the slick stones of winding streets.

Nature has provided Funchal with wonderful trees and flowers. There are hydrangeas, banana trees, oleanders, hibiscus and hundreds of semitropical plants. The finest man-made display comes on New Year's Eve. Then the harbor mirrors not only the lights of the city, but also a fireworks display that has become world famous. The colored streaks of rockets and the sprays of bursting stars rise from the entire curve of the shore and from hills and terraces. Sirens, ships' whistles and church bells provide the din to welcome the new year.

All over the island the nimble fingers of Madeira women create the embroideries and laces that are a major product. They spend spare hours after work in the fields in their homes or on the doorsteps of little white-walled thatched huts in the country embroidering. The finished product is brought to the export houses where it is washed and prepared for the market.

Madeira wine is made from the grapes grown on mountain terraces. When they are brought to the vats in deep wide-topped baskets strapped on men's backs they are crushed by barefooted workers who tramp to the music of a guitar. The wine is aged in the cellars of the wine lodges before it is blended, put in casks and shipped.

Other industries have sprung up on the island. The making of wickerwork baskets, chairs and other products was started in the village of Camache. The willows are grown near the village and prepared for the weavers. Tropical fruits and flowers are grown for export. Sugar cane brought from Sicily centuries ago is grown on small plots on mountain slopes and in valleys. To water crops, streams that trickle from the high fog-covered peaks and tumble as waterfalls in the forests are diverted to irrigation ditches and the water allotted to each grower.

The Azores, farther north in the Atlantic, are also islands of great natural beauty. They lie along the same latitude, thirty-eight degrees north, as Lisbon. Their nine islands form a chain that spreads almost four hundred miles. Sao Miguel, about forty miles long, is the largest of the group. The smallest is Corvo with a length close to four miles. On their total area of almost a thousand square miles live approximately two hundred and fifty thousand people.

The Portuguese first reached the Azores about 1431. Not until several years later did colonists arrive. Prince Henry the Navigator sent not only Portuguese, but also Flemings, Germans and Moors to form the settlements. Friar Goncalo Velho is credited with having rediscovered Santa Maria, most easterly of the islands. It was he who brought the first colonists and farm animals.

All of the islands are relatively small, but each has a capital, a number of smaller towns, and many plantations. Santa Maria has airports which are extremely important in time of war. Its largest town is Vila do Porto.

The capital of Sao Miguel, the largest island, is Ponta Delgada with a population of nearly twenty-five thousand. Its airport is some distance from the town. Roads leading from it pass through areas where fine pineapples, one of the island's major crops, are grown. In its mountains which are volcanic, many of the old craters have become beautiful lakes. Spas have been built where hot springs and geysers occur in regions of thermal activity. There are also tea and coffee plantations.

The other islands, though of less importance, are devoted to agricultural pursuits. Cattle are raised on most of them. Pico Island has a volcano which frequently has snow on its high summit.

The charm of the Azores lies in its flowers and the quaint customs of its people. Flowers flank many of the roads and grow rank in the forests. Wooden-wheeled ox-carts with wickerwork baskets bring produce to markets. White-walled huts dot the hills and valleys. In some of the coves, whalers still bring their catch. These islanders, isolated by the sea, have not given up old customs that seem quaint in this age of machines.

20 THE REPUBLIC

Street fighting in Lisbon and bombardment of the city by some Portuguese ships lying in the harbor marked the birth of the Republic of Portugal. It is estimated some five hundred people were killed. Early October 5, 1910, the republic was proclaimed. On the previous day King Manuel, his mother and other members of the royal family left the country. When the red and green flag of the republic was run up on the flagstaffs of government buildings the rest of the nation accepted the change. A new era in Portuguese history had dawned.

There had been no general hatred toward the king. Lack of interest in what was taking place and weak action by officials was largely responsible for the overthrow of the Braganzas. Hope for new freedoms and more voice in the government was expressed in some quarters. Some leaders of the revolution were eager for power. Confusion, distrust and demagoguery marked the first few years of republican control.

A temporary government was set up with Teofilo Braga, a radical professor, as the provisional president. Many of the ministers were anticlerical. They demanded a separation of church and state. Laws banning all religious orders were revived. Religious processions, which had been so common in the celebration of saints' days, were also prohibited. Titles of the nobility were abolished. The right to strike was granted. This privilege, so new and untried, was abused at the outset by workers who walked off the job in transportation and the cork industry. Their only reason was to see what it was like to be free to do so.

Elections were held on May 11, 1911, for an assembly to draw up a constitution. More than two hundred members were chosen. By late summer the National Assembly had elected Dr. Manuel de Arriaga Portugal's first constitutional president for a term of four years.

Fortunately President Arriaga, over seventy years old, was not a man with extremely radical ideas. He made many attempts to bring some constructive work out of the various political groups which had formed. Three parties became prominent within the first few months. They were the Evolutionists, Democrats and Unionists. Many individuals with purely selfish interests were seeking key positions and the political atmosphere was turbulent. Arriaga's first cabinet fell two months after it was chosen. Strikes, riots, anticlerical demonstrations and monarchist uprisings were of frequent occurrence. Not until 1913 was a ministry selected by the president that was able to last a full year. It was headed by Dr. Alfonso Costa.

World War I broke in Europe in 1914. Portugal, still allied to England by their centuries-old mutual aid treaty, was willing to live up to the agreement. But a country experiencing strikes, riots and wholesale arrests was not in a position to offer much assistance. General Pimenta de Castro, at the time when the National Assembly was not in session, forced President Arriaga to appoint him prime minister. His cabinet consisted largely of military officers. Then Castro assumed the powers of a dictator until the National Assembly hurriedly met and overthrew his government. The events so completely disheartened Arriaga that he immediately resigned the presidency. Dr. Teofilo Braga took the helm until a successor could be elected.

World War I had taken a more serious turn and the Allies needed help. From the beginning of the war a large number of German ships had been interned in Portuguese ports. They now were confiscated. Germany sent protests. On March 9, 1915, she declared war on Portugal. Austria followed suit. By early 1917 Portuguese troops had moved into a sector of the western front. Others had been sent much earlier to protect the colonies in Africa from any attempt by the Germans to seize them.

After the declaration of war, conditions at home continued to be unsatisfactory. Even while Portuguese soldiers were dying on the battlefields, there were strikes and riots in the larger cities. Political parties seemed unable to unite to face the crisis. Prices soared. Grave shortages arose through supplying the needs of the Allies. Eventually a number of army groups became so dissatisfied with conditions that December, 1917, they drove out President Machado and took over the government. Major Sidonio Pais who headed the army revolt took the powers of a dictator. It seemed that only with such powers could the disruption of the war effort be ended. There was a rash of serious disturbances. But, in time, Pais came to be liked by many factions and conditions improved. Then came the end of the war. On December 14, 1918, it brought the end of the career of Pais. The general was at the railroad station in downtown Lisbon when a young man surged from the crowd and fired shots that were fatal to the dictator.

A new plan had been developing for the return of the monarchy. When a naval officer, Joao do Canto e Castro, took over as provisional president after the assassination of Pais it seemed the time was ripe. Royalist forces were successful in the north and the larger cities of that part of Portugal came under their control. The revolt appeared to be well-timed. The provisional government was on the verge of falling. But a victory by the army, still loyal to the republic, occurred at Monsanto. Immediately support for the royalists fell off and the revolt came quickly to an end.

In late 1919 Antonio Jose de Almeida was elected president. He faced a task that was not an easy one. Riots continued. Ministries fell as soon as they had taken control of the government and the value of Portuguese currency dropped to extreme lows. But President Almeida was the first to serve his full term of office. There were attempts to establish dictatorships and there were bloody revolts. Late in his administration there was a very serious attempt in which a number of political leaders were murdered.

President Almeida was succeeded in 1923 by Manuel Teixeira Gomes and the pattern of strikes, riots, uprisings and short-lived ministries continued. In 1925 Bernardino Machado succeeded him. A great financial scandal involving the Bank of Portugal and counterfeit money was uncovered.

By 1926 the record of the republic had not been an imposing one. Since 1911 there had been six presidents elected to office according to the constitution and more than forty ministries. It was not an encouraging picture. The condition seemed never to improve. A number of army officers decided it was high time to put an end to the parade of ministries and disturbances if Portugal and her colonies were to survive. They planned a revolt. It was led by General Manuel Gomes da Costa in the spring of 1926. Machado was removed as president and a group of three officers took over the reins of government. General da Costa proved himself to be just a gruff soldier incapable of ruling a nation. General Antonio Carmona had da Costa taken into custody and sent to the Azores in exile. General Carmona became provisional president and, in 1928, was elected to the office.

Although Carmona had the powers of dictator he used them with discretion. But he was an army man, not a financial expert or a politician. Serious trouble in the national treasury endangered the nation. He looked about for someone to fill a cabinet post who had a knowledge of such matters. Professor Antonio de Oliveira Salazar of Coimbra University was brought to his attention.

Dr. Salazar had not taken a very important part in politics. The methods used by many of the politicians he had observed did not appeal to him. He was born near Coimbra in 1889. His parents were just average Portuguese. His first ambition had been to prepare for the priesthood. The fall of the monarchy and the anticlerical attitude of the republic diverted him from that goal. Since he lived near Coimbra he attended the great university in that city and chose studies in the field of law and economics. He was a serious-minded student.

A thesis he had prepared dealing with the subject of Portuguese currency brought him to the attention of the faculty. When he graduated he was given a position on the teaching staff.

President Carmona appointed Salazar minister of finance in his cabinet. Salazar quickly became disgruntled by the action of some associates and the limited powers that prevented him the freedom he needed if Portugal's financial ills were to be cured. He resigned. Not many months passed before he was called back by Carmona and given the power he demanded. In 1932 he was made prime minister.

Salazar tackled the financial mess that had handicapped the nation. By the end of his first year as minister of finance he had performed the miracle of balancing the national budget. After his elevation to prime minister he was also given the ministries of war and state. The healthy financial condition he had brought about, a condition which had been unknown for many generations, led to a surplus. This he used for housing for the poor, schools, hospitals, roads and airports. Through schools he planned an intensive war on illiteracy. About eighty per cent of the people then were unable to read or write.

By decree, a new constitution incorporating new ideas was given to the people in 1933. With it came a national labor law. It created what leaders spoke of as the New State. Under the new constitution Portugal became a corporate republic.

In the framework of government a president is elected to serve a term of seven years. He appoints the ministers who are to serve in his cabinet and who are to be responsible to him alone. Power would, as before, be centered in the prime minister. Two legislative bodies were created. The national assembly was made up of members selected by the votes of all Portuguese who are heads of families. A corporative chamber, designed to deal with social and economic matters, consists of representatives of guilds and syndicates. Guilds are businessmen's organizations; syndicates are organizations of workers. The idea behind the New State as designed by Salazar was to place associations above the individual in government. This meant that private desires of the workers or of businessmen must be subordinated to the needs of the state.

The surpluses built up through Salazar's policy of requiring that no department can spend beyond the budget were used in promoting industry and developing the country. In 1938 the corporative chamber approved the use of a large sum for developing an irrigation system. The merchant fleet was built up. More schools and more roads were provided.

During World War II Portugal remained neutral. Lisbon was an open port. By the autumn of 1943 she permitted both the United States and Great Britain to have air bases in the Azores. Prosperity reached an all-time peak since the land became prosperous through supplying some of the needs of foreign powers.

General Carmona served as president until his death in 1951. There were a number of candidates to fill the office. The candidate put forth by the Salazar government was General Francisco Lopes. As election time drew near candidates of other parties dropped out of the race or were barred under suspicion of being Communists. In July the election was held and Lopes won. Critics of Salazar brand these elections as fixed. The peculiar system of block voting by the heads of families does not, according to advocates of free elections, permit the voter any choice.

In the recent election President Lopes did not run for office. Rear Admiral Americo Deus Rodrigues Tomas was elected to succeed him. He was a government candidate. Consequently Dr. Salazar remained as prime minister.

Portugal today has the world's third largest colonial empire. Brazil had been lost in the nineteenth century. During the period of Spanish captivity the greater part of the empire in the East was lost to the Dutch and the English. But an empire with an area many times the area of the mother country remains. The largest possessions are in Africa. These include the Cape Verde Islands, Portuguese Guinea, and the archipelago of Sao Tome and Principe. On the west lies the enormous territory of Angola; on the east, the better developed Mozambique which, though much smaller than Angola, has a larger population. In Asia there are three scattered colonies containing Goa, Damao and Diu and generally known collectively as Portuguese India. Macao, near

Hong Kong, is still in Portuguese hands though it is adjacent to Red China. In southeastern Asia part of the island of Timor is a Portuguese possession.

The mother country is rapidly developing industries to reduce its dependence on imports of essential materials. Illiteracy has been greatly reduced. Both economic and financial conditions are rapidly strengthening the corporate republic. Though the standard of living is not high, the Portuguese people are a happy people and very proud of the beautiful land in which they live.

Accent symbols used ordinarily in Portuguese words have been omitted.

INDEX

Accent symbols used ordinarily in Portuguese words have been omitted.